Mountain Moving
Made Easy

Dr. Yvette Rice

…whosoever shall say unto this mountain

Published by F C Publishing, LLC
P. O. Box 5675
Huntsville, AL 35814
(256) 479-2613
www.fcpublishing.com

Unless otherwise indicated, all Scripture quotations are taken
from the King James Version of the Bible.

Scripture quotations marked *AMP* are from
THE AMPLIFIED BIBLE
Copyright © 1960, 1962, 1963, 1968, 1971, 1972, 1973, 1975,
1977 by The Lockman Foundation. All rights reserved. Used by
permission.

Senior Editor: Sandy Tritt
Cover Design: Daniel Buford
Book Layout: Daniel Buford

Printed in the United States

First printing _____ 2008

    10 9 8 7 6 5 4 3 2 1

Library of Congress Control Number: 2008926791

ISBN–13: 978-0-9755217-5-5
ISBN-10: 0-9755217-5-6

DEDICATION

This book is dedicated first to my heavenly Father, for it is through Him I live and move and have my being. I feel privileged to have been chosen for this assignment.

Secondly, I dedicate this book to my earthly father, the late Mr. Maurice Harris, for encouraging me to pursue the dreams God placed in my heart, even when he did not understand them. For the countless smiles, special snacks, and time he shared with his grandchildren, I am thankful.

CONTENTS

ACKNOWLEDGEMENTS

I give God all of the glory and honor, for without Him, I could do nothing. A loving thank you I extend to my husband, Bishop Sam Rice, Th.D., our children, Sharné and Christopher, and our goddaughters, Teronica and Erica, for their patience, encouragement and support.

Thank you to my mother, Mrs. Annie Harris, and my sister, Minister Gloria Flowers, for believing that I could go forth in teaching the Word of God.

Special acknowledgements go to Daniel Buford for sharing his artistic gifts, as well as to Taleesha Elliott for sharing her attentive eyes for details. Thank you to my spiritual parents, Apostle Maurice (Lady Brenda) Wright, Th.D., for their encouragement and instruction in the things of God, and to the New Genesis Community Church family for their prayers.

Thank you to Frank and Theresa Chase, and Sandy Tritt for their meticulous guidance in the preparation of this book.

Dr. Yvette Rice

RECOMMENDATION

Mountain Moving Made Easy by Dr. Yvette Rice gives thought-provoking insights and valuable information in the area of strengthening your faith and overcoming daily challenges. I have found this God-ordered book is one of excellence that will take you from faith to faith and glory to glory. *Mountain Moving Made Easy* serves as a principle-centered aid for you to receive all that God has for you.

I encourage you to read, study and meditate on this wonderful book. I believe your faith will be increased beyond expectations. I thank God for the wisdom and knowledge He has given to my wife to teach all with an ear to hear and a mind to receive that anything is possible with God.

Bishop Sam Rice, Th.D., Sr. Pastor
New Genesis Community Church
Tanner, Alabama

RECOMMENDATION

Many great books are available to read today that will grow us in our Christian faith. However, I think that *Mountain Moving Made Easy* is one that needs to be put on our list of must-reads. God spoke through the Hebrew writer and said that it is impossible to please Him without faith. Faith is the key to increase in our lives.

Pastor Yvette Rice, Th.D., by the aid and direction of the Holy Spirit, has given us a tool for life enrichment as it pertains to our faith. This is not just another book to read for pleasure alone, but it is a resource to get positive results in our walk with God. *Mountain Moving Made Easy* excellently defines the word "faith." It allows you as a reader to gain proper understanding on a topic that is so critical to your relationship with our Lord.

Many patriarchs in the Bible were challenged by God to use faith to fulfill His vision and mission for their lives. Pastor Rice gives us the nuts and bolts to work this awesome mechanism. She not only tells us what faith is but how to take faith and use it in our everyday lives. *Mountain Moving Made Easy* leads you down a clear faith-walking path. Pastor Rice constantly adds color to the picture, eventually exposing you to the destination you expected. She does this by using four principles of mountain-moving faith.

As you read *Mountain Moving Made Easy*, you will start to experience each principle in your everyday life. One principle leads to the next, giving you a sense of spiritual direction as you proceed.

Pastor Rice has given us an instrument to use for a faith release and manifestation in our lives. *Mountain Moving Made Easy* is one book you should read and use as a teaching aid for this generation and others to follow. SHALOM,

Apostle Karockas Watkins, Th.D., Ph.D.,
General Overseer
Emmanuel Church International
Huntsville, Alabama

RECOMMENDATION

Pastor Yvette Rice, Th.D., is one of God's obedient and anointed prophets. She serves as a vessel through which God speaks, and she lives her life by the light of the Word.

Pastor Rice's God-inspired book, *Mountain Moving Made Easy,* has turned my life around. If you are looking for a life-enhancing "how to" book on faith, *Mountain Moving Made Easy* is for you. For the beginner, Pastor Rice uses simple and practical references that point to God for mountain-moving faith. For the more mature Christian, she provides thought-provoking references as a tool to plant and water seed through the prompting of the Holy Spirit.

Mountain Moving Made Easy speaks life, love, power and faith. Thank you, Pastor Rice, for following the prompting of the Holy Spirit.

Dr. Amanda Goodson
Never The Same (NTS) Ministries
Tucson, Arizona

INTRODUCTION

And Jesus answering saith unto them, Have faith in God. For verily I say unto you, That whosoever shall say unto this mountain, Be thou removed, and be thou cast into the sea; and shall not doubt in his heart, but shall believe *that those* **things which he saith shall come to pass; he shall have whatsoever he saith.**

Mark 11:22-23

How do you respond to life's obstacles? Do you speak *about* the troubles you face in life, or do you speak *to* them? Are you a mountain mover, or are you a mountain climber? Did you know that while you are waiting for God to deal with the many situations you face in life, He expects you to stand in the place of authority He has given to you and tell those mountains to get out of your way? *"...If ye have faith as a grain of mustard seed, ye shall say unto this mountain, Remove hence to yonder place; and it shall remove; and nothing shall be impossible unto you"* (Matthew 17:20).

Growing up as a young believer in Christ, I never truly understood the concept of faith; neither did I understand that without faith, I could not please God. We sang songs of climbing mountains but not ones of speaking to them. Like many others, I grew up thinking that if God wanted things to happen in my life, then it was totally up to Him. If this were true, everyone would be saved and be a part of His kingdom; that is His ultimate desire for each of us. I must admit that during those early years as a born-again believer, reading the Bible was not a top priority in my life. In fact, for many years, I did not take my Bible with me to worship services. Like many other books in our home, my Bible sat on the bookshelf and collected dust.

It is amazing to think that as an heir of the Kingdom of God, I had no idea I had an inheritance or how to receive it. This

Truth was revealed to me in Romans 8:17 *AMP*: *"And if we are [His] children, then we are [His] heirs also: heirs of God and fellow heirs with Christ [sharing His inheritance with Him]; only we must share His suffering if we are to share His glory."* I did not understand what it meant to be considered one of God's sons born to a royal family whose kingdom has no end.

> *For in Christ Jesus you are all sons of God through faith. For as many [of you] as were baptized into Christ [into a spiritual union and communion with Christ, the Anointed One, the Messiah] have put on (clothed yourselves with) Christ. There is [now no distinction] neither Jew nor Greek, there is neither slave nor free, there is not male and female; for you are all one in Christ Jesus. And if you belong to Christ [are in Him Who is Abraham's Seed], then you are Abraham's offspring and [spiritual] heirs according to promise* (Galatians 3: 26-29 *AMP*).

What sparked a desire in me to understand the biblical principles of faith and in how to receive that which is rightfully mine? I began to notice others living in God's favor. It was as if life's obstacles and situations moved on their command. As I explored the Word of God, it became apparent that God is not a respecter of persons, but He is a respecter of faith: *"...I now perceive and understand that God shows no partiality and is no respecter of persons, But in every nation he who venerates and has a reverential fear of God, treating Him with worshipful obedience and living uprightly, is acceptable to Him..."* (Acts 10:34-35 *AMP*). It is God's desire that I live an abundantly fulfilled life, the same as any of His other children.

Spoken by Jesus in John 10:10 *AMP*, we are told: *"The thief comes only in order to steal and kill and destroy. I came that they may have and enjoy life, and have it in abundance (to the full, till it overflows)."* I discovered the difference between those who have and those who have not is the understanding and application of the Word of God in their lives. Matthew 13:12 *AMP* expresses it in this manner: *"For whoever has [spiritual knowledge], to him will more be given and he will be furnished richly so that he will have abundance; but from him who has not, even what he has will be taken away."*

God has given us His Word, The Holy Bible, as our road map for daily living. This is clearly explained to us in 2 Timothy 3:16-17 *AMP*:

> *Every Scripture is God-breathed (given by His inspiration) and profitable for instruction, for reproof and conviction of sin, for correction of error and discipline in obedience, [and] for training in righteousness (in holy living, in conformity to God's will in thought, purpose, and action), So that the man of God may be complete and proficient, well fitted and thoroughly equipped for every good work.*

Mountain Moving Made Easy was inspired by the Holy Spirit to aid believers in the understanding and application of four basic principles found in God's Word relative to operating by faith in the Kingdom of God. Over the next twelve chapters, we will study the importance of establishing these principles in our lives on a daily basis: (1) Having the Faith of God (2) Speaking to the Mountains (3) Believing (4) Expecting to Receive.

The ability to understand and live by these four principles does not rest in our own strength, but in the Power of God on the inside of us. Emphatically stated in Ephesians 3:20, we see that it is by the Power of the Holy Spirit that we rise up in faith as mountain movers: *"Now unto Him that is able to do exceeding abundantly above all that we ask or think, according to the power that worketh in us."*

This faith to move mountains is achieved only when we come to God with a repentant heart (a change of mind in how we live and think) and accept Jesus the Christ, the only begotten Son of God, as our way into the Kingdom of God. We must not only accept Jesus as our Savior (Deliverer), we must also declare Him our Lord (Owner). If you have not already taken this step in your life, a detailed explanation of God's redemptive plan is included throughout the contents of this book. An opportunity to confirm your understanding and acceptance of Christ as your Savior and Lord is provided in "Experiencing the Kingdom of God" on page 115.

It is my sincere prayer that by the transforming Power of the Holy Spirit, stagnation in your life will become a part of your past. Whether there are mountains of fear, failure, regret, depression, anxiety, sickness or poverty standing in your way or you simply desire greater knowledge and understanding relative to operating in faith in the Kingdom of God, I invite you to read on to discover how to move those mountains and go forth.

PRINCIPLE ONE
HAVE THE FAITH OF GOD

Chapter 1
Defining Faith

"...If you have faith (a firm relying trust) and do not doubt, you will not only do what has been done to the fig tree, but even if you say to this mountain, Be taken up and cast into the sea, it will be done."

Matthew 21:21 *AMP*

The word "mountain" used in Matthew 21:21 is derived from the Greek word "*ŏrŏs*" meaning "...proverbially, of overcoming difficulties, or accomplishing great things."[1] Overcoming those obstacles or mountains in our lives does not depend upon our own merit or ability, but on whether we operate in the faith apportioned to us by God. Several accounts are recorded in scripture where Jesus relates challenges or circumstances to mountains: Matthew 17:14-20 (a man's demoniac son), Matthew 21:18-21 and Mark 11:12-23 (a non-producing fig tree). In each scenario, an activity against the Kingdom of God had taken place on earth and having faith was the first requirement in bringing forth a solution.

While studying the first principle given to us regarding life as a mountain mover, I pondered the footnotes from Mark 11:22 that expounded on the translation of the original Greek text. I verified this note with other references, and each of them read the same. Instead of the verse just stating "Have faith in God," the footnotes included the statement "Have the faith of God." These two sentences are similar, yet there is a distinct difference. We are required to not only have faith in God; we must have the faith of God as well. Contemplating this command that we should have the faith of God, the Holy Spirit, our Teacher, directed me to Hebrews 6:13. *"For when God made promise to Abraham, because He could swear by no greater, he swore by himself."* God, the creator of all things, knew there was no one greater to trust in than Himself. Written in Genesis 22:16, we find the same declaration: *"...By myself have I sworn, saith the Lord..."* Having the God kind of faith indicates our absolute trust must remain in the Lord, for there is none greater to rely upon. When we function with the faith of God, we will acquire the promises of God.

Let us now seek to expand our understanding concerning faith. Hebrews 11:1 describes faith the following way: *"NOW FAITH is the substance of things hoped for, the evidence of things not seen."* As a child in my local church congregation, I heard this scripture read many times. Unfortunately, I still did not have a clear understanding of the definition of the word "faith." Many times in an effort to define or describe a word, we make statements like: "it *is* pretty," "it *is* orange" or "it *is* strong." These are attributes of the subject, but a statement of what the word actually means is not given. In a similar way, I could tell you ice cream *is* satisfying to the appetite and it *is* cold to the tongue, but I still did not define the word "ice cream": "a sweet variously flavored frozen food containing cream or butterfat and usually eggs."[2]

Returning to Hebrews 11:1, it was only when I researched the word "faith" in *Strong's Expanded Exhaustive Concordance Of The Bible* did I comprehend the definition. In the Concordance, the word "faith" is translated from the Greek word *"pistis"* [pis´-tis] meaning, "persuasion, i.e. credence; moral conviction (of religious truth, or the truthfulness of God)."[3] The word *"pistis"* originates from another Greek word *"pĕithō,"* [pi´-tho] meaning "to rely (by inward certainty), persuade, trust, obey, have confidence, believe, agree."[4] In other words, faith is an absolute, immoveable trust in God and His Word. We have to be strong in confidence that whatever the Lord proclaims through His Word, *it is so!* God's Word is the final authority for every situation in our lives. Simply stated, faith is living by absolute trust in God and His unchangeable Word.

In a culture such as the United States of America which operates under a democratic system of government, it is a difficult task to consider a law of any kind as final or unchangeable. As U. S. citizens, we have grown accustomed to seeking to change anything we do not agree with. The problem with this concept is that the Laws of God (His Word) were established in a kingdom (The Kingdom of God) where whatever was decreed by the King (Jesus, The King of kings) was unchangeable. This is why it is necessary that we repent [have a change of heart (mind) towards sin and opposing the way of the Lord] before we can understand or live victoriously as a citizen of the Kingdom of God. *"From that time Jesus began to preach, crying out, Repent (change your mind for the better, heartily amend your ways, with abhorrence of your past sins), for the kingdom of heaven is at hand"* (Matthew 4:17 *AMP*).

As with any true kingdom, the citizens of that kingdom trust and obey their king. The citizens know their well-being rests totally in the hands of their king: *"Fear not, little flock; for it is your Father's good pleasure to give you the kingdom"* (Luke 12:32). They also understand and accept that whatever the king has decreed as law is unchangeable. There is nothing to vote on or discuss with the intentions of amending what has been written. Faith is an absolute, unmovable trust in our King and His Word, making it the final authority for our lives.

The word "faith" in Galatians 3:26, is from the same word *"pistis"* found in Hebrews 11:1, and is used to describe our relationship with Jesus. However, in this context, it is used with regards to a saving faith or our trusting Christ, the Messiah, as our Savior and the only way (entrance) into the Kingdom of God: *"For ye are all the children of God by faith in Christ Jesus."*

Now that we understand the definition of faith in accordance with the Greek dictionary of the New Testament, let us begin to examine attributes of faith. According to Hebrews 11:1, God is telling us faith is *right now*. It is not a delayed reaction. When our requests are made known to God, our faith must be activated instantaneously. Therefore, every minute of every day, we must function in the faith of God. Romans 1:17 declares that the just (God's people) must live each day by faith: *"For therein is the righteousness of God revealed from faith to faith: as it is written, The just shall live by faith."* The *Amplified Bible* extrapolates Romans 1:17 in this manner:

> *For in the Gospel a righteousness which God ascribes is revealed, both springing from faith and leading to faith [disclosed through the way of faith that arouses to more faith]. As it is written, The man who through faith is just and upright shall live and shall live by faith.*

Once we activate the faith process in our lives, it should be ever increasing or developing into greater faith. We must consistently live by absolute trust in God's Word.

I began to realize faith must be seen as a lifestyle and not just a tool we use during a crisis. This revelation has been a progressive experience in my life. At the age of 23, I was hired as an engineer for a federal agency in the southern United States. The career choice I made required at times a great deal of travel. Six weeks into my new job, I was sent to a class in Los Angeles, California. I must give you a clearer picture of my situation. I had traveled with my family and friends, but I had never traveled that far away from home alone. I grew up in a small town in Alabama, approximately 60,000 people. The largest roadway I had driven on was a typical four-lane interstate. It was close to sunset when I arrived at the largest airport I had ever seen in my life. I was expected to rent a car and drive on what appeared to be twenty lanes of traffic! That was an exaggeration; it was probably six lanes on each side, but that was more than enough for a small town girl like me.

On the way to the hotel, I suddenly became very religious. Unfortunately, God was not seeking religion from me; He was seeking a true relationship with someone who trusted Him in every aspect of his or her life. Even though I had been attending worship services, that lifestyle had not yet manifested. Over an hour and many mumbled words of prayer later, I arrived at the hotel. I could not have been happier to find a Gideon's Bible tucked in the nightstand in my hotel room. I actually read it for over an hour, meditating on Psalm 23. Frightened and alone, I quoted that scripture nightly until the fear in me dissipated.

Regrettably, when I returned home safely and the crisis was over, I put the constant reading of the Word of God aside for several more years. Of course I continued attending worship services regularly, but daily *study* (not just reading) of the Word of God and prayer on a continual basis was not in my schedule. (The key is you cannot fit God into your schedule; He must be the center of your schedule and everything else must work around Him.) This is the problem with many who claim to be believers of Christ. They religiously attend worship services, not realizing that God is not impressed by more religious people such as the Pharisees or those spoken of in James 1: 23–26 *AMP* who practice all kinds of outward rituals, yet whose hearts and lives are not a reflection of one who knows Christ the King. God is seeking those who truly desire a relationship with Him, one that is more than outward appearances:

> *For if anyone only listens to the Word without obeying it and being a doer of it, he is like a man who looks carefully at his [own] natural face in a mirror; For he thoughtfully observes himself, and then goes off and promptly forgets what he was like. But he who looks carefully into the faultless law, the [law] of liberty, and is faithful to it and perseveres in looking into it, being not a heedless listener who forgets but an active doer [who obeys], he shall be blessed in his doing (his life of obedience). If anyone thinks himself to be religious (piously observant of the external duties of his faith) and does not bridle his tongue but deludes his own heart, this person's religious service is worthless (futile, barren)* (James 1:23-26 *AMP*).

I now realize my first major experience away from home was orchestrated by God to start me on a journey of faith and of learning the importance of a consistent lifestyle in the study of His Word.

Let us again examine Hebrews 11:1. We can now say, daily trust in the Word of God *"... is the substance of things hoped for..."* The word "substance" originates from the Greek word *"hupŏstatsis"* [hoop-os'-tas-is], meaning "a setting under (support)."[5] This word originates from another Greek word *"hupŏ,"* indicating "the agency or mean, through."[6] Our trust in the Word of God is the agency or means for the things we hope to physically appear in our lives. Absolute trust in the promises of God makes the invisible visible. We receive the physical manifestation of God's promises on Earth from that which has already been given to us in Heaven when we live by faith. *"NOW FAITH is the assurance (the confirmation, the title deed) of the things [we] hope for, being the proof of things [we] do not see and the conviction of their reality [faith perceiving as real fact what is not revealed to the senses]"* (Hebrews 11:1 *AMP*). Hebrews 11:3 (KJV) further explains: *"Through faith we understand that the worlds were framed by the Word of God, so that things which are seen were not made of things which do appear."*

We must remember we are now citizens of the invisible Kingdom of God because of our repentance and trust in the Lord Jesus. *"Jesus answered him, I assure you, most solemnly I tell you, that unless a person is born again (anew, from above), he cannot ever see (know, be acquainted with, and experience) the kingdom of God"* (John 3:3 *AMP*).

In that brief experience 25 years ago, I knew God's peace and presence abided in that hotel room because I read His Word nightly. I trusted the Lord to protect me and return me home safely because His Word had become the confirmation and proof that I was not alone.

Another attribute of faith is its ability to shield us. In our stand against the wiles of Satan, the "shield of faith" is included as an essential piece of defensive armor in what the Apostle Paul calls the "whole armor of God." Ephesians 6:16 states: *"Above all, taking the shield of faith, wherewith ye shall be able to quench all the fiery darts of the wicked."* The word "faith" applied in Ephesians 6:16 is the same Greek word *"pistis"* found in Hebrews 11:1. The Apostle Paul tells us that above everything else, we must take up the shield of faith (complete trust in the promises of God) regardless of the missiles of doubt, sickness, disease or any other trial the devil may fire toward us. Our position is one of standing faithfully with our shield up [the Word of God], knowing that the physical manifestation of victory promised to us from our Father and established in His Kingdom is assured: *"...Our Father Who is in heaven, hallowed (kept holy) be Your name. Your Kingdom come, Your will be done on earth as it is in heaven"* (Matthew 6: 9b-10 *AMP*).

Chapter 2
Increasing Your Faith

So faith comes by hearing [what is told], and what is heard comes by the preaching [of the message that came from the lips] of Christ (the Messiah Himself).

Romans 10:17 *AMP*

In Romans 12:3, we are told that each one of us has been given the measure of faith by God: *"For I say, through the grace given unto me, to every man that is among you, not to think of himself more highly than he ought to think; but to think soberly, according as God hath dealt to every man the measure of faith."* The word "measure" comes from the Greek word "*mĕtrŏn*" [met'ron], meaning "a limited portion, (degree)."[7] We should note the scripture says we are given "the" and not "a" measure of faith. The word "the" denotes a particular amount, meaning that each one of us begins with an equal portion of faith.

There are occasions in the Bible when Jesus commended His followers for exercising great faith when seeking Him with a request: Matthew 8:5-10 (the centurion's servant healed) and Matthew 15:21-28 (the healing of the Canaanite woman's daughter). In Matthew 8:5-11, Jesus admired the maturity of the centurion's faith. In fact, Jesus stated He had not seen this kind of faith in all of Israel: *"When Jesus heard it, he marvelled, and said to them that followed. Verily I say unto you, I have not found so great faith, no not in Israel"* (Matthew 8:10). It must be noted that the centurion was not a Jewish descendant of Abraham (verse 11); however, his understanding of the governmental authority of a kingdom became apparent when he asked Jesus to "speak the word only" to bring healing to his servant (verse 8). The centurion understood that when a king speaks a word, it becomes law and cannot be contradicted or changed. This centurion acknowledged Jesus as King.

According to *The New Strong's Exhaustive Concordance*, the word "great" noted in Matthew 8:10 is interpreted "so vast as this, i.e. such (in quantity, amount, number or space) – *"tŏsŏutŏs"* [tos-oó-tos]."[8] The word "great" used by Jesus to characterize the faith of the Canaanite woman in Matthew 15:28 is the origin of our English word "mega." This Greek word *"megas"* [meg´-as] is defined as "great, exceedingly, high, large, mighty."[9]

In agony from the thought of her daughter being tormented by a demon, the Canaanite's request was first denied by our Lord. *"...Have mercy on me, O Lord, thou Son of David; my daughter is grievously vexed with a devil. But He answered her not a word..."* (Matthew 15:22-23a). Yet with undeniable persistence, the woman continued to make her supplication known to Christ. The immense magnitude of the Canaanite's faith in Jesus won His attention: *"Then Jesus answered and said unto her, O woman, great is thy faith: be it unto thee even as thou wilt. And her daughter was made whole from that very hour"* (Matthew 15:28). Twice in her conversation with Jesus, the Canaanite woman referred to Him as "Lord." The word "Lord" actually acknowledges Jesus as One of supreme authority. The Canaanite declared Jesus to be her Master and Owner regardless of the fact she was not an Israelite. Like the centurion, this woman understood that as her Master, Jesus was obligated to meet her needs.

Mountains of anxiety and fear are explored in Matthew 6:25-30 (concerns over provisions) and Matthew 8:23-26 (the fear of perishing in a dangerous storm). In both scenarios, Jesus, denoting the disciples' lack of trust in His ability, spoke the words "little faith." Combined, these two words make up the Greek word *"ŏligŏpistos"* [ol-ig-op´-is-tos], "lacking confidence (in Christ) – literally, this word means of little faith and is used only by the Lord as a tender rebuke."[10]

Recognizing that each of us began with *"the measure of faith"* and God is no respecter of persons (Acts 10:34), it is obvious that we are responsible for the maturing or growth of our faith. How do we progress from "little faith" to faith that moves mountains? The answer is found in Romans 10:17: *"So then faith cometh by hearing, and hearing by the word of God."* *The Amplified Bible* translates this verse accordingly: *"So faith comes by hearing [what is told], and what is heard comes by the preaching [of the message that came from the lips] of Christ (the Messiah Himself)."*

While meditating on this particular scripture, I pondered the message Jesus preached. The Holy Spirit directed me to Mathew 4:17: *"From that time Jesus began to preach, and to say, Repent: for the kingdom of heaven is at hand."* The central message of Jesus' earthly ministry was the Gospel of the Kingdom of God. *"But He said to them, I must preach the good news (the Gospel) of the kingdom of God to the other cities [and towns] also, for I was sent for this [purpose]"* (Luke 4:43 *AMP*). When I searched *The New Strong's Expanded Exhaust Concordance of the Bible*, there were over 135 references collectively in the books of Matthew, Mark, Luke and John that expounded on the words spoken from the lips of Jesus relevant to the Kingdom of Heaven or the Kingdom of God.

Matthew 13:1-23 acquaints us with a parable regarding a farmer who sowed seed in the ground with the expectations of harvesting a significant crop. Jesus then relates the seeds the farmer sowed to the Word of God. In Matthew 13:18-19 *AMP*, Jesus specifically refers to the Word of God as the "Word of the kingdom": *"Listen then to the [meaning of the] parable of the sower: While anyone is hearing the Word of the kingdom and does not grasp and comprehend it, the evil one comes and snatches away what was sown in his heart. This is what was sown along the roadside."*

Recalling our discussion in chapter one pertaining to the importance of every word decreed by a king, we determined that these words are unchangeable and considered law once they are spoken. Relative to the Kingdom of Heaven, the Word of the kingdom that the evil one (Satan) seeks to seize or take by force is crucial to the development of our faith. As citizens of the Kingdom of God, we cannot read the Bible with a democratic mentality. We must establish in our minds that we are reading the "Word of the Kingdom." If there is no hearing and understanding of the Word our King has decreed and declared as law in His kingdom, our ability to trust Him as One who is our faithful Lord is nonexistent. *"Forever, O Lord, thy word is settled in heaven. Thy faithfulness is unto all generations: thou hast established the earth, and it abideth. They continue this day according to thine ordinances, for all are thy servants"* (Psalm 119:89-91).

In Matthew 13:31-32 *AMP*, Jesus explains more about the Kingdom of Heaven as He compares it to the growth process of a grain of mustard seed. He describes the grain of mustard seed as the least of all seeds; yet, it grows and becomes the greatest among the garden herbs. In fact, it develops into a tree large enough to house the fowl of the air on its branches:

> *Another story by way of comparison He set forth before them, saying, The kingdom of heaven is like a grain of mustard seed, which a man took and sowed in his field. Of all the seeds it is the smallest, but when it has grown it is the largest of the garden herbs and becomes a tree, so that*

the birds of the air come and find shelter in its branches.

This same comparison is given in Mark 4:20-33; however, in Mark, Jesus refers to the Kingdom as the "Kingdom of God" instead of the Kingdom of Heaven.

Later in Matthew 17:20, Jesus compares our faith to a grain of mustard seed. Many people have misquoted this passage of scripture by saying "If you have faith *the size of* a mustard seed." It actually reads, *"...If ye have faith as a grain of mustard seed, ye shall say unto this mountain, Remove hence to yonder place; and it shall remove; and nothing shall be impossible unto you."* The word "as" denotes a comparison. The size of the seed is not as significant as the growth process of the seed. Jesus wanted the disciples to understand that our faith, like the seed, must grow daily. Mustard trees are known to grow ten feet or more. They are also known to experience rapid growth. As we hear and comprehend the Word of the kingdom, we will transition from faith that is small to faith that moves mountains.

Consistent with this teaching, *The Amplified Bible* extrapolates Matthew 17:20b in the following way: *"...For truly I say to you, if you have faith [that is living] like a grain of mustard seed, you can say to this mountain, Move from here to yonder place, and it will move; and nothing will be impossible to you."* Key words in this passage of scripture are *"that is living."* If anything is alive, it should be growing and increasing.

In retrospect, the great faith of the centurion soldier and the Canaanite woman were possibly generated by what they heard about Jesus.

And Jesus went about all Galilee, teaching in their synagogues, and preaching the gospel of the kingdom, and healing all manner of sickness and all manner of disease among the people. And his fame went throughout all Syria: and they brought unto him all sick people that were taken with divers diseases and torments, and those which were possessed with devils, and those which were lunatic, and those that had the palsy; and he healed them. And there followed him great multitudes of people from Galilee, and from Decapolis, and from Jerusalem, and from Judea, and from beyond Jordan (Matthew 4:23-25).

Revisiting Romans 10:17 (*"faith cometh by hearing, and hearing by the Word of God"*), we can see the significance of what we hear. There are many sounds coming forth from the world into our ears on a continual basis. What comes through our ears penetrates our hearts. That sound (or thought) then flows from our hearts (minds) and is spoken out of our mouths. These characteristics are mentioned in Matthew 12:34b: *"...out of the abundance of the heart, the mouth speaks."* A continuous cycle is generated by the words we speak. If the Word of the Kingdom has not been the sound transmitted from our ears into our minds, the foundation for our belief system has been established from erroneous information. If that belief system is formulated from the ideology of the world's system—the practices and ideas of mankind without God's instruction—it will produce doubt and unbelief instead of faith and absolute trust in the Word of God. *"For my thoughts are not your thoughts, neither are your ways my ways, saith the Lord. For as the heavens are higher than the earth, so are my ways higher than your ways, and my thoughts than your thoughts"* (Isaiah 55: 8-9). God's thoughts are not carnal or stirred by human emotions. Unlike mankind, which gathers its thoughts from what is seen upon the earth with the natural eye, faith speaks the eternal thoughts of God, that which is not seen.

The Lord tells us in Matthew 4:17 *AMP* to repent: *"change your mind for the better, heartily amend your ways, with abhorrence of your past sins."* Romans 12:2 *AMP* reiterates the importance of changing our minds for the better with God's Word:

> *Do not be conformed to this world (this age), [fashioned after and adapted to its external, superficial customs], but be transformed (changed) by the [entire] renewal of your mind [by its new ideals and its new attitude], so that you may prove [for yourselves] what is the good and acceptable and perfect will of God, even the thing which is good and acceptable and perfect [in His sight for you].*

The word "transform" originates from the Greek word *"metamorphŏō,"* meaning "to change into another form…the obligation being to undergo a complete change which, under the power of God, will find expression in character and conduct."[11] The English word "metamorphosis" is a derivation of this Greek word. Examining nature as God created it, a caterpillar must undergo a metamorphosis to become a butterfly. Accordingly, our minds actually go through a transformation process as we read the Bible, changing us from one with carnal thoughts to one who functions in great faith as a citizen of the Kingdom of God.

Not only is our faith affected by the words we hear, but also by the information we read. One night as I sat reading the scriptures and praying, I asked the Lord about the passage: *"…faith cometh by hearing."* I wanted to know if this passage of scripture included the reading of God's Word. The Lord then instructed me to read the words silently. As I studied, I realized as I read silently, the words echoed in my brain the same as if spoken aloud. We add information to our belief systems by the words we read and hear. If it is the Word of God we are hearing or reading, we are increasing our faith.

The word "hearing" translates from the Greek word "*akŏē*" [ak-ŏ-ay], meaning "... (the act, the sense or the thing heard)...report, which ye heard, preached."[12] This word "*akŏē*" originates from another Greek word, "*akŏuō*" [ak-oó-o], meaning "come (to the ear), be noised, be reported, understand."[13] The key to the transformation of our minds is not just hearing, but also understanding what we hear.

In the fourth chapter of Mark, Jesus teaches us to pay attention to what we hear relative to the teachings of God. Mark 4:23-25 *AMP* says:

> *If any man has ears to hear, let him be listening and let him perceive and comprehend. And He said to them, Be careful what you are hearing. The measure [of thought and study] you give [to the truth you hear] will be the measure [of virtue and knowledge] that comes back to you—and more [besides] will be given to you who hear. For to him who has will more be given; and from him who has nothing, even what he has will be taken away [by force].*

In other words, successful application of the scriptures we hear depends upon how much thought and study we give to those scriptures after we have heard them.

Often times we take notes as the Word of God is taught. However, very few of us actually meditate on the notes at a later time. We must study the message provided for us, seeking a clear understanding of the application of that message as it relates to our everyday walk with the Lord. A daily regimen of purposeful Bible study produces total mind renewal. The once erroneous belief system is transformed into the scriptural foundation necessary for mountain-moving faith. Remember, faith comes by hearing God's Word. A prosperous mind, one that is saturated with the Truth of the scriptures, will produce an abundant life, including good health: *"Beloved, I wish above all things that thou mayest prosper and be in health, even as thy soul prospereth"* (3 John: 2).

In a similar manner, if we lack understanding or give minimal study to the Word of God we hear, the adversities of life will cause us to forfeit the knowledge that leads to a victorious lifestyle. According to the thirteenth chapter of Numbers, twelve men were sent to spy out the land of Canaan for the Israelites. All of them heard the same promises of God pertaining to their victorious inheritance; however, only Joshua and Caleb heard and understood what they were told. Exercising their faith, Joshua and Caleb made a decision to go in and possess the land.

Doubt was generated in the hearts of the other ten spies because they had not given adequate care to the promises of God they had heard. Their response was based only on what they saw with their natural eyes. They allowed fear, which is the opposite of faith, to consume them and force the promises of God from their hearts, resulting in their confession, "We be not able." *"And Caleb stilled the people before Moses, and said, Let us go up at once, and possess it; for we are well able to overcome it. But the men that went up with him said, We be not able to go up against the people; for they are stronger than we"* (Numbers 13:30-31).

True faith goes beyond the visible and gathers its information from God's Word, which is spoken from the invisible Kingdom of Heaven; this is where great hosts of angels and the supernatural, miracle-working Power of God assure us the victory. Forty years later the victory at Canaan was manifested as Joshua, being led by God, escorted the next generation of Israelites around Jericho, causing the walls of the city to collapse supernaturally (Joshua 6:1-27).

The parable of the sower and his seed in Matthew 13:18-21 *AMP* also reinforces the importance of guarding the Word of the Kingdom in our hearts:

> *Listen then to the [meaning of the] parable of the sower: While anyone is hearing the Word of the kingdom and does not grasp and comprehend it, the evil one comes and snatches away what was sown in his heart. This is what was sown along the roadside. As for what was sown on thin (rocky) soil, this is he who hears the Word and at once welcomes and accepts it with joy; Yet it has no real root in him, but is temporary (inconstant, lasts but a little while); and when affliction or trouble or persecution comes on account of the Word, at once he is caused to stumble [he is repelled and begins to distrust and desert Him Whom he ought to trust and obey] and he falls away.*

Again, it is obvious to us that it is the Word of the Kingdom that Satan seeks to devour or remove from our hearts. If the devil can get you to distrust the King by not accepting His Word as the unchangeable Truth, then he can cause you to lose your inheritance.

When we have opportunities to hear God's Word recorded we should take advantage of them. Even the secular world recommends repetition as a method of influencing our thoughts. As we listen to the Word over and over again, we set an atmosphere for tremendous growth in the realm of faith. Do not forget the growth process of the grain of mustard seed. It grows by the nurturing of the elements, such as sunlight and rain. This concept also applies to our faith. The Son-Light (The Word [John 1:1-14]), along with the Holy Spirit (our Teacher [John 14:26]), provides the spiritual nutrition conducive to mature faith. The more of God's Word we hear and study, the greater our faith becomes.

In Joshua 1:8 *AMP*, the Lord instructs Joshua to meditate on His word day and night: *"This Book of the Law shall not depart out of your mouth, but you shall meditate on it day and night, that you may observe and do according to all that is written in it. For then you shall make your way prosperous, and then you shall deal wisely and have good success."* "Meditate" is the crucial word in this passage of scripture. Translated from the Hebrew word *"hâgâh"* [haw-gaw'], "meditate" implies "to mutter, speak, study or talk."[14] To be successful, we must hear ourselves speak the Word of God. When communicating, we pay attention to ourselves more than anyone we come in contact with. It cannot be emphasized too much: faith comes when we hear and understand God's Word.

The word "cometh" used in Romans 10:17 is translated from the Greek word *"ĕk,"* denoting "origin (the point whence motion or action proceeds), from."[15] For simplification purposes only, let us make a substitution in this passage: *so then faith originates or proceeds from hearing the Word of God.* It is that simple: *no Word, no faith!*

If I were to ask you whether or not you had faith to deal with a pending challenge in your life right now, would you be able to give me scripture from the Word of God to support a victorious outcome? For most believers, the answer is "no." After studying a passage of scripture in Genesis 8:22, it became apparent to me that if I intend to receive a bountiful harvest in my life, I must plant seed. *"While the earth remaineth, seedtime and harvest, and cold and heat, and summer and winter, and day and night shall not cease."* If I desire a harvest of apples, I must plant apple seeds.

Re-examining the parable of the sower, the type of seed (The Word) we must plant in our hearts is determined by the area of need, challenge or mountain we are facing. If the mountain is sickness, we need to plant healing seed or scriptures. *However, you should not wait until trouble comes to begin planting seed. Plant God's Word today! The farmer plants early, expecting a harvest at the time of need.*

Chapter 3
According To Your Faith

And when Jesus departed thence, two blind men followed him, crying, and saying, *Thou Son of David*, have mercy on us. And when he was come into the house, the blind men came to him: and Jesus saith unto them, Believe ye that I am able to do this? They said unto him, Yea, Lord. Then touched he their eyes, saying, According to your faith be it unto you.

Matthew 9:27-29

Reading this passage of scripture, we see that God is not a respecter of persons; however, He is a respecter of faith. In Matthew 9: 27-29, it is the *action* of the two blind men that brought forth their miracle. They followed Jesus, crying out to Him for their healing. When He asked them if they believed He was able to heal them, they responded in faith: *"Yea, Lord."* Jesus' reply was: *"According to your faith be it unto you."* Faith is a requirement for the Lord to manifest His promises in our lives.

Making a request to the Lord with confidence in His ability to provide the answer is an act of faith. James 4:2b *AMP* states, *"...You do not have, because you do not ask."* Many times when it comes to petitioning the Lord, we hold back, thinking we are undeserving or unworthy to ask anything from Him. Unfortunately, this misconception has developed throughout the Body of Christ because of lack of knowledge of the Word of the Kingdom. To ask anything of the Lord requires that we know we have been given that privilege by the scripture planted in our hearts. 1 John 5: 14-15 *AMP* tells us:

And this is the confidence (the assurance, the privilege of boldness) which we have in Him: [we are sure] that if we ask anything (make any request) according to His will (in agreement with His own plan), He listens to and hears us. And if (since) we [positively] know that He listens to us in whatever we ask, we also know [with settled and absolute knowledge] that we have [granted us our present possessions] the requests made of Him.

We know that God's will for us is expressed in His Word. Therefore, when we pray according to the scripture, we are praying God's will, and with confidence, we make the Word of God the evidence of our expected answer from the Lord.

According to Luke 11:9 *AMP*, our King has given us an open invitation to make our request known to Him: *"So I say to you, Ask and keep on asking and it shall be given you; seek and keep on seeking and you shall find; knock and keep on knocking and the door shall be opened to you."* Translating the word "ask" resulted in a surprising definition. The word *"aitĕō"* [ahee-teh-o], meaning "to ask as a child from a parent," is connected to the word *"punthanŏmai,"* meaning "a demand of something due."[16] What could we possibly have due to us from God?

God has promised us all the benefits of our salvation and becoming a citizen of the Kingdom of God (Romans 10: 9), including deliverance, protection, healing and wholeness. There are so many other promises in the Word of God, however, I cannot list them all in the contents of this book. The significant point is that we have been given permission to go to our Father in Heaven with the petitions of our hearts.

While studying the book of Luke one night, I pondered the thought of being told by God, *"Ask and keep on asking."* Although the word "persistence" came to mind, my thoughts raced back to my childhood years. Growing up as a child of hard-working parents, I knew my mother and father did their very best to meet my needs. I asked my parents for something I desired for school. A few days later, an even greater need materialized. I was reluctant to go back and ask my parents again, because I knew they had recently spent money on me. While recalling that experience, I realized that with God, we should not feel guilty about making our many requests known; our Father in Heaven has an endless supply of anything we may need. Our inheritance will never run out; our Heavenly Father has no lack; and His desire to see our needs met is even greater than that of our earthly parents. Therefore, we can ask and keep on asking Him without guilt or reluctance.

In Esther 4:11, we are given the proper protocol for approaching the throne of a king: *"All the king's servants, and the people of the king's provinces, do know, that whosoever, whether man or woman, shall come unto the king into the inner court, who is not called, there is one law of his to put him to death, except such to whom the king shall hold out the golden scepter, that he may live..."* This means that death is inevitable for the one who approaches the king's throne uninvited. We can rejoice however, because Christ our King has held out His scepter to us indefinitely.

Emphatically stated in Hebrews 4:16 *AMP*, we are told to be bold in our coming unto the throne of grace:

> *Let us then fearlessly and confidently and boldly draw near to the throne of grace (the throne of God's unmerited favor to us sinners), that we may*

> *receive mercy [for our failures] and find grace*
> *to help in good time for every need [appropriate*
> *help and well-timed help, coming just when we*
> *need it].*

As defined in the Greek dictionary of the New Testament, the word "boldly" or "*parrhēsia*," pronounced *par-rhay-seé-ah,* means "*all out-spokenness,* i.e. *frankness, bluntness, publicity*; by imp. *assurance.*"[17] For many, approaching God in prayer with such assurance may seem arrogant. A lack of understanding of kingdom principles in the Word of God has generated this erroneous belief. However, if we have scripture as the foundation for our request, we can exercise our faith in knowing we have a blood-bought right to approach the throne. We can rejoice in knowing that we have the grace of God's unmerited favor extended to us for every need in our lives. Just as the blind men in Matthew 9:27-29, the action of our faith assures us we will receive an answer from the Lord.

The writer of Hebrews 10:19-22 confirms that we have full access to enter into the presence of God (the Holy of Holies) to commune and fellowship with our Heavenly Father, receive forgiveness for our sins and make our requests known to Him:

> *Having therefore, brethren, boldness to enter*
> *into the holiest by the blood of Jesus, By a new*
> *and living way, which he hath consecrated for*
> *us, through the veil, that is to say, his flesh; And*
> *having an high priest over the house of God; Let*
> *us draw near with a true heart in full assurance*
> *of faith, having our hearts sprinkled from an evil*
> *conscience, and our bodies washed with pure*
> *water.*

In *The Amplified Bible,* Philippians 4:6 reads, *"Do not fret or have any anxiety about anything, but in every circumstance and in everything by prayer and petition (definite requests), with thanksgiving, continue to make your wants known to God."* We should be specific in making our requests as well as free from fear and reservations when petitioning God. Translated, the word "request" originates from the Greek word *"aitĕō,"* meaning "to ask."[18] This is the same word used in Luke, chapter 11.

We are warned when making requests to be sure our motives are pure. God will withhold answers He knows will bring destruction to our lives.

> *You are jealous and covet [what others have] and your desires go unfulfilled; [so] you become murderers. [To hate is to murder as far as your hearts are concerned.] You burn with envy and anger and are not able to obtain [the gratification, the contentment, and the happiness that you seek], so you fight and war. You do not have, because you do not ask. [Or] you do ask [God for them] and yet fail to receive, because you ask with wrong purpose and evil, selfish motives. Your intention is [when you get what you desire] to spend it in sensual pleasures* (James 4:2-3 *AMP*).

Remember, the lust of the flesh (desiring that which belong to others) is one of Satan's weapons. We must be able to discern in our hearts if we have pure motives. If we are not sure, we may ask God to reveal our motives to us, according to James 1:5-6a: *"If any of you lack wisdom, let him ask of God, that giveth to all men liberally, and upbraideth not; and it shall be given him. But let him ask in faith."*

Faith requires us to take action. Accordingly, James 2:17 in *The Amplified Bible* tells us, *"So also faith, if it does not have works (deeds and actions of obedience to back it up), by itself is destitute of power (inoperative, dead)."* Recalling Matthew 17:20 in *The Amplified Bible*, our faith must be, "living like a grain of mustard seed." Emphasizing the word "living," it is time for us to take action in steps of obedience to God's Word and act on that which we believe God will bring to pass.

Six months after my husband Sam and I were married, we sought the Lord's blessing about purchasing our first home. After a brief search, we agreed we had found the perfect house. Although the asking price was more than we anticipated, we knew it was the will of God for us to have that particular house.

Sam and I prayed about the offer we should propose for the house. One day while we were working, 25 miles apart, God distinctly spoke a particular dollar amount to each of us. Later that evening, my husband mentioned what God had spoken to him. Amazingly, it was the same amount God had spoken to me.

Our offer was rejected, but my husband and I did not waiver from what we knew our King had spoken. Almost a month later, on the day we received our earnest money back in the mail, our real estate agent called us. Just as God had promised, the couple changed their minds, and they decided to accept our offer. In fact, they even paid most of the closing costs. Although our offer was substantially lower than the asking price, if we had not acted in faith, we would not be enjoying our home today.

We are given a list of biblical patriarchs who are recognized for their acts of faith in Hebrews 11:4-39. I have often referred to these verses as the "Faith Hall of Fame." God found each of these patriarchs worthy to be named because of their acts of obedience. I consider each one of them mountain movers. The bold acts of two of these patriarchs, Abraham and Rahab, are included in James

2:21-26 *AMP*:

> *Was not our forefather Abraham [shown to be] justified (made acceptable to God) by [his] works when he brought to the altar as an offering his [own] son Isaac? [Genesis 21:1-14.] You see that [his] faith was cooperating with his works, and [his] faith was completed and reached its supreme expression [when he implemented it] by [good] works. And [so] the Scripture was fulfilled that says, Abraham believed in (adhered to, trusted in, and relied on) God, and this was accounted to him as righteousness (as conformity to God's will in thought and deed), and he was called God's friend. You see that a man is justified (pronounced righteous before God) through what he does and not alone through faith [through works of obedience as well as by what he believes]. So also with Rahab the harlot—was she not shown to be justified (pronounced righteous before God) by [good] deeds when she took in the scouts (spies) and sent them away by a different route? [Joshua 2:1-21.] For as the human body apart from the spirit is lifeless, so faith apart from [its] works of obedience is also dead.*

In verses 21 and 25 respectively, Abraham and Rahab took action based on their faith. Both proved their trust in God through sacrificial acts of obedience, Abraham in offering his son, Isaac, and Rahab in placing her own life in danger for the safety of God's men.

The word "works" found in the second chapter of the

book of James is translated from the Greek word "*ĕrgŏn*" [eŕ-gon], meaning "...toil (as an effort or occupation); by impl. an act: - deed, doing, labor, work."[19] This word is also applied in John 14:10-14 by Jesus to describe the ministry He has given us to do on the earth. It is our *true occupation* to do the works of Christ, operating in faith by the Power of the Holy Spirit.

> *Believest thou not that I am in the Father, and the Father in me? The words that I speak unto you I speak not of myself: but the Father that dwelleth in me, he doeth the works. Believe me that I am in the Father, and the Father in me: or else believe me for the very works' sake. Verily, verily, I say unto you, He that believeth on me, the works that I do shall he do also; and greater works than these shall he do; because I go unto my Father. And whatsoever ye shall ask in my name, that will I do, that the Father may be glorified in the Son. If ye shall ask any thing in my name, I will do it* (John 14:10-14).

In Romans 12: 4-8, we are told we are one body in the Lord, and He has given each one of us spiritual gifts for ministering. It is when we all function together that we represent our Lord on the earth as He desires. This directive requires us to operate those gifts by faith in the Power of the Holy Spirit, duplicating the works of our Lord. God has put a demand on us, as the Body, to live by faith. It is by faith we lay hands on the sick and expect their healing to manifest. It is by faith we cast out demons. It is by faith we prophesy, speaking forth the mysteries of the Kingdom of God. Miracles are performed through us as we operate in faith.

For as we have many members in one body, and all members have not the same office: So we, being many, are one body in Christ, and every one members one of another. Having then gifts differing according to the grace that is given to us, whether prophecy, let us prophesy according to the proportion of faith; Or ministry, let us wait on our ministering: or he that teacheth, on teaching; Or he that exhorteth, on exhortation: he that giveth, let him do it with simplicity; he that ruleth, with diligence; he that showeth mercy, with cheerfulness (Romans 12:4-8).

In Matthew 17:14-20, Jesus' disciples were asked to heal a man's son struck with epilepsy that was caused by an evil spirit. They were unable to heal him. As a result, the man carried his son to Jesus. Jesus' response was one of rebuke toward His disciples: *"...O faithless and perverse generation, how long shall I be with you? how long shall I suffer you? bring him hither to me"* (v.17). Jesus wanted the disciples to know He would not always be with them physically on the earth. It was time for them to take action in the faith that should have developed while Jesus was with them.

Jesus taught the disciples the Word of God and trained them by example. After the disciples asked Jesus why they were not able to cast out the evil spirit, He reminded them the life we live is a constant walk of faith. *We* must act in faith. *We* must speak to the mountain. *We* must believe we have the authority to do what Jesus did upon the earth.

Another example of faith in action is given to us in Luke 5:3-7 *AMP*:

And getting into one of the boats, [the one] that

belonged to Simon (Peter), He requested him to draw away a little from the shore. Then He sat down and continued to teach the crowd [of people] from the boat. When He had stopped speaking, He said to Simon (Peter), Put out into the deep [water], and lower your nets for a haul. And Simon (Peter) answered, Master, we toiled all night [exhaustingly] and caught nothing [in our nets]. But on the ground of Your word, I will lower the nets [again]. And when they had done this, they caught a great number of fish; and as their nets were [at the point of] breaking, They signaled to their partners in the other boat to come and take hold with them. And they came and filled both boats so that they began to sink.

You may be a minister called by God to win souls to the Kingdom, yet your congregation is not growing. You may be a businessman or businesswoman desiring to increase your profits to prevent bankruptcy, but the economy has created a slow down in product demand. Maybe you are a young man or woman who continues to run into a brick wall as you seek a college education or deliverance from addictions or other destructive habits. Right now, you may be saying: "Lord, I have toiled all night, yet I see no results." God would have me say to you: "Cast your nets into the deep one more time with the Word of God to back you up." Do not forget, God has promised to provide *"appropriate help and well-timed help, coming just when you need it"* (Hebrews 4:16b *AMP*).

In this hour, God is looking for those who will represent Him and His Kingdom in excellence upon the earth. He is seeking those who will act in faith, according to His Word, demonstrating a living faith in your city, state, nation and this world. Will you be the "whosoever" that goes forth in faith in the name of the Lord Jesus? Will you choose to be the one to say: "Yes, I will lay hands on the sick, I will cast out demons. I will win souls until Jesus returns. I am 'more than a conqueror,' and I will victoriously occupy the earth until Jesus returns. I will stand in faith as part of the Body of Christ and do the will of the Father."

Chapter 4
Love, the Energizer of Faith

For [if we are] in Christ Jesus, neither circumcision nor uncircumcision counts for anything, but only faith activated *and* energized *and* expressed *and* working through love.

Galatians 5:6 *AMP*

Reading the title of this chapter, you may ask, "What does love have to do with faith?" A family member of mine told me she enrolled in a class on faith at her church. During this time in her life, forgiveness was a great challenge for her. In fact, she said God had sent many people to minister to her about the unforgiveness she harbored toward her former husband. One evening after class, the instructor approached her with a prophetic word from the Lord telling her that unforgiveness was hindering His plans for her life. She, in frustration, replied to the teacher, "I thought this was a class on faith." The instructor responded, "Yes, but faith works by love."

In retrospect, not only does Mark 11:25-26 give us instructions for moving mountains, it also includes a stipulation requiring forgiveness. *"And when ye stand praying, forgive, if ye have aught against any: that your Father also which is in heaven may forgive you your trespasses. But if ye do not forgive, neither will your Father which is in heaven forgive your trespasses."*

In *The Amplified Bible*, Mark 11:25 is expressed in this manner: *"And whenever you stand praying, if you have anything against anyone, forgive him and let it drop (leave it, let it go), in order that your Father Who is in heaven may also forgive you your [own] failings and shortcoming and let them drop."*

Some of the mountains that have been resistant in our lives could be weighted down by unforgivingness. Many times we say we have forgiven others for pains or frustrations they have caused us, yet we continue to replay the offense in our minds or in conversations with others. The significant instruction given to us in Mark 11:25 *AMP* is: *"...let it drop, leave it, let it go..."* We must release those offenses because they could be detrimental to our ability to become mountain movers.

In ministry, the occasion for exercising forgiveness can be frequent. There are so many different personalities and temperaments among those in the Kingdom of Heaven.

> *Again the Kingdom of Heaven is like a dragnet which was cast into the sea and gathered in fish of every sort. When it was full, men dragged it up on the beach, and sat down and sorted out the good fish into baskets, but the worthless ones they threw away. So it will be at the close and consummation of the age. The angels will go forth and separate the wicked from the righteous (those who are upright and in right standing with God) and cast them [the wicked] into the furnace of fire...* (Matthew 13: 47-50 *AMP*).

Satan seeks out opportunities to plant those who live for him among local flocks so he can cause dissension and division in the Body of Christ. Remember, verse 49 states that some of the fish caught in the net were thrown away at a later time; this means there are those who are not of the sheepfold of Christ hidden in the midst of some congregations. There are also different stages of spiritual maturity within any local congregation; therefore, opportunities for testing by God relative to forgiveness are immense. As a pastor, I cannot allow my emotions to affect my love walk. According to 1 Corinthians 13, love is not an emotion; it is an act of the will.

Early in ministry, I faced serious hurt and rejection because I was a female called to the ministry in a particular local church. I knew God had wonderful plans for my husband and me; however, there were many barriers to overcome. I wrote down some promises I heard God speak to me in my quiet time with Him. I began to travail in prayer for the manifestations of those promises to come forth, yet no answers seemed to materialize. I thought I was praying the prayer of faith about our situation until the Lord showed me I was carrying unforgiveness in my heart. I had to release emotions of rejection, hurt and offense that I had harbored towards those I felt had caused me afflictions. Once I refused to allow the devil to continue to replay those past pains in my mind, I chose to forgive, and the mountains began to move out of the way.

Jesus demonstrated immense compassion toward people as He walked upon the earth. His compassion for those He ministered to was motivated by love. I finally realized that unforgivingness, strife or anger in my heart could prevent me from praying in faith for those who need healing or deliverance. This is important when serving in ministry or desiring to be used of God. We are tested when those who cause hurt in our lives come to us for prayer or consolation. Imagine the sorrow in the heart of our Lord as He looked from the cross and said: *"...Father, forgive them; for they know not what they do"* (Luke 23:34a). In 1 Thessalonians 5:8, we are encouraged to remain calm, wearing the breastplate of faith and love as we go forth, accomplishing the will of God: *"But let us, who are of the day, be sober, putting on the breastplate of faith and love; and for a helmet, the hope of salvation."*

Recalling Ephesians 6:16, love is added to the shield of

faith as a defense weapon. It has been stated that fear can be seen as "False Evidence Appearing Real." In 1 John 4:18, we can see that we should not allow fear to hinder us in acts of obedience: *"There is no fear in love; but perfect love casteth out fear: because fear hath torment. He that feareth is not made perfect in love."* We cannot allow the fear of being hurt again keep us from obedience to God. Knowing that God is love and that He has love beyond measure for us will erase any hurt we may encounter along the road to becoming God's mountain movers.

The Amplified Bible extrapolates 1 John 4:18a the following way: *"There is no fear in love [dread does not exist], but full grown (complete, perfect) loves turns fear out of doors and expels every trace of terror!"* The breastplate of faith and love blocks fear from entering our hearts. Whether it is fear of failure in our lives or fear related to the pains of relationships in the home, church or workplace, faith and love working together are the eliminator. It is by recognizing the exceeding greatness of God's love that we can place absolute trust in Him and His word. God's Word tells us to "fear not." How do we go forth in faith without fear? It is by the love of God through Jesus Christ.

The Apostle Paul ends his letter to the Ephesian Church in chapter six by giving a blessing of peace and love joined with faith. He reminds them that faith and love are interrelated: *"Peace be to the brethren, and love joined with faith, from God the Father and the Lord Jesus Christ (the Messiah, the Anointed One)"* (Ephesians 6:23 *AMP*). The word "love" expressed in each of these scriptures comes from the Greek word "*agapē*," meaning "affection or benevolence; spec (plur.) a love feast."[20] This love is unconditional; it is given even if it is not reciprocated.

First Corinthians 13:1-3 *AMP* is pertinent in understanding the relationship between faith and love.

If I (can) speak in the tongues of men and [even] of angels, but have not love (that reasoning, intentional, spiritual devotion such as is inspired by God's love for and in us), I am only a noisy gong or a clanging cymbal. And if I have prophetic powers (the gift of interpreting the divine will and purpose), and understand all the secret truths and mysteries and possess all knowledge, and if I have [sufficient] faith so that I can remove mountains, but have not love (God's love in me) I am nothing (a useless nobody).

We can have enough faith to move mountains, yet, if God's love in us is not the energizer of that faith, we are useless in the Kingdom of God. Recognizing love as a crucial ingredient in our quest to become mountain movers, we must understand this word from a biblical perspective.

Love endures long and is patient and kind; love never is envious nor boils over with jealousy, is not boastful or vainglorious, does not display itself haughtily. It is not conceited (arrogant and inflated with pride); it is not rude (unmannerly) and does not act unbecomingly. Love (God's love in us) does not insist on its own rights or its own way, for it is not self-seeking; it is not touchy or fretful or resentful; it takes no account of the evil done to it [it pays no attention to a suffered wrong]. It does not rejoice at injustice and unrighteousness, but rejoices when right and truth prevail. Love bears up under anything and everything that comes, is ever ready to believe the

*best of every person, its hopes are fadeless under
all circumstances, and it endures everything
[without weakening]* (1 Corinthians 13:4-8
AMP).

We casually use the word "love" to express our emotions
toward others without grasping God's requirements. God's love is
unconditional as well as an act of the will. We have to choose to
live with the love of God in our hearts or minds. It is our choice
whether we receive it or extend it to others.

Now that we understand the love of God as defined in
1 Corinthians 13:4-8, let us now observe its effects on faith. If
our faith is energized by God's love, the following conditions will
prevail:

- We shall patiently wait for the promises
  of God to manifest because God's love
  gives us power to endure.

- When we see mountains moved, we will
  not become prideful but make sure that
  all the glory goes to God because we
  operate through His Power and not our
  own.

- We will not use faith selfishly; we will
  desire to see mountains moved for others
  because God's love does not tolerate self-
  seeking motives.

- Unforgivingness will not be a hindrance
  in moving mountains because God's love

pays no attention to wrong treatment or offenses.

- We will not grow weak in faith because the love of God bears up under any situation or circumstance and will never fail.

Going forth with mountain moving faith energized by love, we will be able to endure and fulfill the destinies God has prepared for us. What happened to the family member that had to learn to forgive? The mountain of divorce was cast into the sea, and the marriage Satan thought he had destroyed was restored through Jesus Christ. In fact, she and her husband are involved in Kingdom Business for God.

Chapter 5
Faith, Not Presumption

Then some of the traveling Jewish exorcists (men who adjure evil spirits) also undertook to call the name of the Lord Jesus over those who had evil spirits, saying, I solemnly implore *and* charge you by the Jesus Whom Paul preaches! Seven sons of a certain Jewish chief priest name Sceva were doing this. But [one] evil spirit retorted, Jesus I know and Paul I know about, but who are you?

Acts 19:13-15 *AMP*

According to *Webster's New Collegiate Dictionary*, presumption is defined as "an attitude or belief dictated by probability."[21] In the same dictionary, the word "probability" is defined as "the chance that a given event will occur."[22] A study of the word "chance" provides us with the following definition: "something that happens unpredictably without discernible human intention or observable cause ... the possibility of an indicated or a favorable outcome in an uncertain situation."[23] Evaluating these definitions, we find speculative words such as "probability," "chance," "unpredictability" and "uncertain." It would be safe to say that presumption involves arriving at a conclusion based on *non-factual information* or assumptions. In fact, the word "presume," a derivative of presumption, can be defined as "to suppose to be true without proof."[24]

Deficiency in the understanding of the Word of God has caused many in the Body of Christ to misinterpret presumption for faith. As defined previously, we know that faith is absolute trust in God and His Word. We have also ascertained that God's Word is our evidence or proof that what we believe will be the final outcome even though it has not yet manifested. Presumption is characterized by forming opinions and assumptions for a final outcome without substance or truthful evidence to support those opinions.

An excellent biblical example of faith versus presumption can be found in Acts 19: 11-16:

> *And God wrought special miracles by the hands of Paul: So that from his body were brought unto the sick handkerchiefs or aprons, and the diseases departed from them, and the evil spirits went out of them. Then certain vagabond Jews, exorcists, took upon them to call over them which had evil spirits the name of the Lord Jesus, saying, We adjure you by Jesus Whom Paul preacheth. And there were seven sons of one Sceva, a Jew, and chief of the priests, which did so. And the evil spirit answered and said, Jesus I know, and Paul I know; but who are ye? And the man in whom the evil spirit was leaped on them, and overcame them, and prevailed against them, so that they fled out of that house naked and wounded.*

Seeing the results the Apostle Paul achieved while casting out demons in the name of the Lord Jesus, the seven sons of Sceva sought a similar outcome. The Apostle Paul operated by *faith* in the Word of God. He understood the authority that had been given to him as a citizen of the Kingdom of Heaven. The Apostle Paul was filled with the Holy Spirit, and he knew that casting out demons was one of the signs of the believers spoken of in the

Gospel of Mark 16:15-18:

> *And he said unto them, Go ye into all the world,*
> *and preach the gospel to every creature. He that*
> *believeth and is baptized shall be saved; but he*
> *that believeth not shall be damned. And these*
> *signs shall follow them that believe; In my name*
> *shall they cast out devils; they shall speak with*
> *new tongues; They shall take up serpents; and*
> *if they drink any deadly thing, it shall not hurt*
> *them; they shall lay hands on the sick, and they*
> *shall recover.*

The seven sons of Sceva were Jewish men who did not know the Lord Jesus as their Savior and King. Although these sons were known as exorcists (those who seek to drive out demonic spirits), they were not operating as believers in Christ as written in the Book of Mark, chapter 16. The sons of Sceva sought to cast out demons *based on Paul's revelation of Christ and not their own.* These self-proclaimed exorcists did not accomplish the same results because they were not operating in faith, but in presumption.

Biblical faith requires knowledge of the Word of God. Remember faith comes by hearing and understanding God's Word. Presumption is based upon what is seen with the natural eye or through inconclusive evidence. This is apparent in verse 15 when the evil spirit answered back, acknowledging Jesus' authority and the authority Christ had given Paul, but had neither knowledge of nor fear of the seven sons of Sceva. They were not citizens of the Kingdom of Heaven; therefore, the power to do what Jesus commissioned did not apply to them.

Another biblical example of presumption can be found in

the Book of Acts 28:3-6:

> *And when Paul had gathered a bundle of sticks,*
> *and laid them on the fire, there came a viper out*
> *of the heat, and fastened on his hand. And when*
> *the barbarians saw the venomous beast hang on*
> *his hand, they said among themselves, No doubt*
> *this man is a murderer, whom, though he hath*
> *escaped the sea, yet Vengeance suffereth not to*
> *live. And he shook off the beast into the fire, and*
> *felt no harm. Howbeit they looked when he should*
> *have swollen, or fallen down dead suddenly: but*
> *after they had looked a great while, and saw no*
> *harm come to him, they changed their minds, and*
> *said that he was a god.*

Recapitulating the life of the Apostle Paul, the barbarians
were presumptuous in thinking that he was a murderer or an evil
person. Many Christians believe that another brother or sister in
the Lord is in sin if they are faced with tragedy or tribulation. In
the Gospel of John 16:33 *AMP*, Jesus cautions us we will face
various trials in this life. Consequently, He does not indicate these
trials come because of sin we have committed:

> *I have told you these things, so that in Me you may*
> *have [perfect] peace and confidence. In the world*
> *you have tribulation and trials and distress and*
> *frustration; but be of good cheer [take courage;*
> *be confident, certain, undaunted]! For I have*
> *overcome the world. [I have deprived it of power*
> *to harm you and have conquered it for you].*

As a citizen of the Kingdom of God, we have inherited a victorious outcome despite anything the natural or physical evidence may indicate. Based on the Word of the Kingdom, expecting victory is not an assumption, but truth.

The barbarians spoken of in the Book of Acts 28:3-6 were not aware of this promise of our Lord, neither did they have knowledge of the truth given to us in Luke 10:19: *"Behold, I give unto you power to tread on serpents and scorpions, and over all the power of the enemy: and nothing shall by any means hurt you."* This scripture did not give the Apostle Paul permission to become a snake handler or charmer, but it did give him the confidence to know he would not be harmed. In Acts 28:6, the Apostle was able to shake off the viper in faith, knowing the Lord had promised if he touched a serpent or came in contact with anything deadly, it would not harm him.

Throughout the Body of Christ, many saints of God seek to obtain or achieve things based on presumption and not faith. Those operating in faith succeed because of absolute trust in God's Word and obedience in that which God has commissioned. Those operating in presumption fail many times in similar efforts because they go forth based on what they see others do, assuming that if something worked in one ministry it will work in another. Psalm 127:1 tells us, *"EXCEPT THE Lord build the house, they labour in vain that build it...."* If God does not plant the vision, the work is done in vain.

During my husband's sixth year as a senior pastor of a local congregation, the Lord gave him the vision for a ministry that would be called New Genesis. God told him his seventh year in ministry would be a year of completion or perfection for him, and in the eighth year He would give him a new beginning. Although other pastors had already started new ministries during my husband's sixth year of pastoring, the Lord's instructions were explicit on which year the manifestation of the promise would take place. My husband could not assume that since God had promised him a new start, he could go ahead and resign at an earlier time.

Two years later, in 2002, the Lord commissioned my husband to go forth. God also sent a visiting minister to preach a message to us from Genesis 26:15-24, entitled "It Is Time To Dig Another Well." This message correlated with the circumstances surrounding the call God had given us. It was confirmation that we were hearing the Lord correctly and that it was the proper time for our departure. Obedient to the call of God, The New Genesis Community Church was organized and incorporated in March 2002. It was in my husband's eighth year of ministry as a senior pastor, exactly as the Lord had said.

Understanding numbers from the perspective of the Jewish culture, the number eight symbolizes a new beginning (Ezekiel 43:27, 1 Peter 3:20). The Book of Genesis is the first book of the Bible. "*Genesis* is a Greek word meaning, 'origin,' 'source,' 'generation,' or 'beginning.'" [25] We acted in faith, not presumption, and we had the Word of God to back us up. Although we know that God is not a respecter of persons, God's timing must be considered when acting on the Lord's Word: *"TO EVERTHING there is a season, and a time for every matter or purpose under heaven"* (Ecclesiastes 3:1 *AMP*).

Many people find themselves in the bondage of debt because of presumption. They see others driving new automobiles, wearing new designer clothes or building new homes. In an effort to do the same things, they make foolish purchases and unwise decisions based on the presumption "God did it for them, He will do it for me" or "I make more money than they do. I know I can afford a new home, etc., if they can." What God has done for others should not be the basis for what we expect to come forth in our lives. As believers, there are factors we should consider before we make important decisions:

(1) Are we living a life of faith or presumption?

(2) Have we placed ourselves in a position to be the recipient of God's favor by tithing faithfully: *"Bring ye all the tithes into the storehouse, that there may be meat in mine house, and prove me now herewith, saith the Lord of hosts, if I will not open you the windows of heaven, and pour you out a blessing, that there shall not be room enough to receive it"* (Malachi 3:10).

(3) Have we sown according to God's instructions so that we can receive a harvest: *"Give, and [gifts] will be given to you; good measure, pressed down, shaken together, and running over, will they pour into [the pouch formed by] the bosom [of your robe and used as a bag]. For with the measure you deal out [with the measure you use when you confer benefits on others], it will be measured back to you"* (Luke 6:38 *AMP*).

(4) Are those things we seek from God pertinent to His plans for our lives or are we striving to satisfy our own fleshly desires?

Revisiting the "Faith Hall of Fame" in Hebrews 11:4, we see that Abel was prompted by faith to offer a better sacrifice to the Lord than his brother Cain: *"By faith Abel offered unto God a more excellent sacrifice than Cain, by which he obtained witness that he was righteous, God testifying of his gifts: and by it he being dead yet speaketh.* " The word "excellent" used in Hebrews 11:4 is translated from the Greek word "*plĕiōn*" [pli-own], meaning "more in quantity, number, or quality; ...the major portion."[26] Many have interpreted that God accepted Abel's offering as one of faith because Abel gave the majority or best portion to the Lord.

A detailed account of the story of the two brothers, Cain and Abel, can be found in the Book of Genesis 4: 3-8 *AMP*:

> *And in the course of time Cain brought to the Lord an offering of the fruit of the ground. And Abel brought of the firstborn of his flock and of the fat portions. And the Lord had respect and regard for Abel and for his offering. But for Cain and his offering He had no respect or regard. So Cain was exceedingly angry and indignant, and he looked sad and depressed. And the Lord said to Cain, Why are you angry? And why do you look sad and depressed and dejected? If you do well, will you not be accepted? And if you do not do well, sin crouches at your door; its desire is for you, but you must master it. And Cain said to his brother, Let us go out to the field. And when they were in the field, Cain rose up against Abel his brother and killed him.*

After a more comprehensive study of this incident, it is evident that not only did Abel offer his *firstlings* to the Lord, he gave it with the right attitude and spirit (a heart of thanksgiving and faith). His brother Cain offered fruit of the ground; however, sin appears to be hidden in his heart. Envy, covetousness and jealousy cannot be the motivation for us asking or seeking from the Lord. James 2:3 is a clear warning about harboring evil in our hearts as we come before our Heavenly Father.

An omnipotent (all-knowing) God warned Cain that sin closely awaited him. This sin is specifically mentioned in 1 John 3:12 *AMP*: *"[And] not be like Cain who [took his nature and got his motivation] from the evil one and slew his brother. And why did he slay him? Because his deeds (activities, works) were wicked and malicious and his brother's were righteous (virtuous)."*

As believers going forth in our daily walk with God we must ask ourselves: Are we operating in faith or presumption? Are our acts of faith based upon what God has said in His Word, or are we acting upon what we have seen occurring in the lives of others?

PRINCIPLE TWO
SPEAK TO THE MOUNTAINS

Chapter 6
Created in the Image of God

**God said, Let Us [Father, Son, and, Holy Spirit]
make mankind in Our image, after Our likeness,
and let them have complete authority over the fish
of the sea, the birds of the air, the [tame] beasts,
and over all of the earth, and over everything that
creeps upon the earth.**

Genesis 1:26 *AMP*

A critical factor in living this life as a mountain mover
is understanding and accepting who we are in Christ
Jesus. I included the word "accepting" in the previous statement
because many of us have poor images of ourselves. Pain and
disappointment from the past or current difficulties accepting
ourselves can prevent us from realizing how God has dynamically
created each of us. *"I will praise thee; for I am fearfully and
wonderfully made: marvelous are thy works"* (Psalm 139:14a).
While many of us may accept Christ as the way into the Kingdom
of Heaven, very few comprehend the significance of living with
Kingdom citizenship or what it means to be created in the image
and after the likeness of God the Father, Son and Holy Spirit.

God has plans and purposes for each of us, and has given
us benefits and privileges to fulfill those purposes: *"For I know
the thoughts and plans that I have for you, says the Lord, thoughts
and plans for welfare and peace and not for evil, to give you hope
in your final outcome"* (Jeremiah 29: 11 *AMP*). Our lives should
consist of more than rising each day, laboring in a particular
workplace and returning home to watch television and go to bed.

As citizens of the Kingdom of God, we have been empowered by the Holy Spirit to go into those workplaces as world changers, demonstrating that with God all things are possible.

Unfortunately, it has been noted by many pastors and teachers of the Word of God that the wealthiest places in the world are cemeteries because of the people who have died with God's potential for greatness locked up inside them. Ultimately, until we fully grasp who we are in the Lord, those mighty plans God has for each of us will remain unfulfilled.

Recalling Genesis 1:26, it is our spiritual composition that we must consider when operating in faith in the Kingdom of God. Twenty years ago, as a believer, I really did not comprehend who I was in the Lord, therefore I accepted what others had to say about me; that I was a female and I could not be used by God for ministry outside the rearing of our children and teaching or ministering to other women. I was well aware these tasks were very important, yet deep within my soul, I knew I was created by God to do special work for Him to advance His kingdom on the earth. The still voice of the Holy Spirit on the inside of me kept telling me not to settle for what I had been told by others, but to seek my Creator and find out why He placed me on the earth at this specific time and place.

As I read more of the Word of God, the Lord revealed to me that when it comes to His love, salvation, grace and power, there are no distinctions between race, gender or social status. Stated clearly in Galatians 3:28, if I saw myself as an inferior workmanship of the Lord, it was caused by a lack of knowledge on my part: *"There is neither Jew nor Greek, there is neither bond nor free, there is neither male nor female: for ye are all one in Christ Jesus."*

The more time I spent in prayer and fellowship with my Heavenly Father (including prayer and studying the Bible), the more acquainted I became with His glorious power, majesty and love. It became obvious to me that God's attributes and characteristics should be coming forth from me because He is my Father and Creator, and I have His Divine Nature and Authority (DNA). Genesis 1: 27-28 *AMP* expresses this thought:

> *So God created man in His own image, in the image and likeness of God He created him; male and female He created them. And God blessed them and said to them, Be fruitful, multiply, and fill the earth and subdue it [using all its vast resources in the service of God and man]; and have dominion over the fish of the sea, the birds of the air, and over every living creature that moves upon the earth.*

We may ask the question: "What do these scriptures have to do with moving mountains from my life?" According to Genesis 1: 26-28, God has given us dominion over the created elements as well as the authority to use the resources of the earth. What we do with the authority we have been given has everything to do with why those mountains remain before us, continuing to block our paths and hinder us from fulfilling the destinies our Lord has already assigned to us.

By the inspiration of the Holy Spirit, Moses (the author of the Book of Genesis) used two distinct words in Genesis 1:26-28 to describe the actions of God with reference to our existence. Those words are "make" and "created." A study of the word "created" reveals the Hebrew word "*bârâ*" [baw-raw´], which expresses "creation out of nothing; noting this word can only be applied to God as the originator."[27] The word "*âsâh*" [aw-saw´] translates the word "make" as "to form from something that is already created."[28]

In Genesis 1:1, God uses the word "created" to describe the formation of the Heaven and the Earth. Genesis 1:9-10 *AMP* tell us of the creation of the dry land upon the Earth: *"And God said, Let the waters under the heavens be collected into one place [of standing], and let the dry land appear. And it was so. God called the dry land Earth, and the accumulated waters He called Seas. And God saw that this was good (fitting, admirable) and He approved it."* The dry land, including the dust of the ground, was created or formed from nothing that existed.

According to Genesis 2:7 *AMP*, the Lord then took the dust of the ground and made mankind. *"Then the Lord God formed man from the dust of the ground and breathed into his nostrils the breath or spirit of life, and man became a living being."* God used a resource that He created (the dust of the ground) and made mankind, and then He gave mankind authority over His creation and charged us to expand and benefit His kingdom upon the earth.

The word "image" as used in Genesis 1:26 is translated from the Hebrew word *"tselem"* [tseh´-lem], which is defined as "a phantom...resemblance; hence, a representative."[29] In similar descriptive terms, "likeness" comes from the word *"demûth"* [dem-ooth´], and signifies "the original after which a thing is patterned."[30] We have been patterned after our Creator, God the Father, Son and Holy Spirit: *"God said, Let Us [Father, Son, and Holy Spirit] make mankind in Our image, after Our likeness..."* (Genesis 1:26a *AMP*).

John 4:24 *AMP* declares: *"God is a Spirit (a spiritual Being) and those who worship Him must worship Him in spirit and in truth (reality)."* The word "Spirit" translates from the word *"pnĕuma"* means "divine (God)."[31] We are told in 1 Thessalonians 5:23 that God created man as a triune being. We are a spirit (like

God), we possess a soul, and we live in a physical body: *"And the very God of peace sanctify you wholly: and I pray God your whole spirit and soul and body be preserved blameless unto the coming of our Lord Jesus Christ."* After researching the word "spirit" applied in 1 Thessalonians 5:23, I determined it is the same word *"pnĕuma"* written in John 4:24. *"Pnĕuma,"* as it applies to mankind, means "superhuman."[32]

In Christ Jesus, we are not just natural, but we are supernatural beings because God Himself resides on the inside of us. We must perceive ourselves as *pnĕuma*—non-carnal, invisible, with power the way God sees us. We must determine that the real mountain mover is that powerful spirit-being created in the image and after the likeness of our Father and Creator, God.

> *Consequently, from now on we estimate and regard no one from a [purely] human point of view [in terms of natural standards of value]. [No] even though we once did estimate Christ from a human viewpoint and as a man, yet now [we have such knowledge of Him that] we know Him no longer [in terms of the flesh]. Therefore if any person is [ingrafted] in Christ (the Messiah) he is a new creation (a new creature altogether); the old [previous moral and spiritual condition] has passed away. Behold, the fresh and the new has come! But all things are from God, Who through Jesus Christ reconciled us to Himself [received us into favor, brought us into harmony with Himself] and gave to us the ministry of reconciliation [that by word or deed we might aim to bring others into harmony with Him]* (2 Corinthians 5:16-18 AMP).

The fall of mankind through the first man, Adam, caused us (mankind) to no longer perceive ourselves as that powerful non-carnal spirit-being God made. The sin brought through Adam contaminated our spirits, causing us to forget who we were created to be and what we were originally created to accomplish on earth. Thus our contaminated mind or soul began to control us, pulling us further from our initial existence.

> *AND YOU [He made alive], when you were dead (slain) by [your] trespasses and sins in which at one time you walked [habitually]. You were following the course and fashion of this world [were under the sway of the tendency of this present age], following the prince of the power of the air. [You were obedient to and under the control of] the [demon] spirit that still constantly works in the sons of disobedience [the careless, the rebellious, and the unbelieving who go against the purposes of God]. Among these we as well as you once lived and conducted ourselves in the passions of our flesh [our behavior governed by our corrupt and sensual nature], obeying the impulses of the flesh and the thoughts of the mind [our cravings dictated by our senses and dark imaginings]. We were then by nature children of [God's] wrath and heirs of [His] indignation, like the rest of mankind* (Ephesians 2: 1-3 *AMP*).

The Holy Spirit has recreated us into the supernatural human that was God's original intent because we have accepted Jesus as our Savior and Lord. However, it is now necessary for our minds or intellect to catch up with our regenerated spirits. Mind renewal in accordance with the Word of God is necessary, because the poor carnal image we had of ourselves before our restoration in Christ now hinders what God desires to accomplish through us on earth. It is our newly regenerated spirit that must rule our intellect or minds because mountains are not moved by emotions; they are moved by faith working through the Power of the Holy Spirit as He operates through us.

> *Thus it is written, The first man Adam became a living being (an individual personality); the last Adam (Christ) became a life-giving Spirit [restoring the dead to life]. But it is not the spiritual life which came first, but the physical and then the spiritual. The first man [was] from out of earth, made of dust (earthly-minded); the second Man [is] the Lord from out of heaven. Now those who are made of dust are like him who was first made of the dust (earthly-minded); and as is [the Man] from heaven, so also [are those] who are of heaven (heavenly-minded), And just as we have borne the image [of the man] of dust, so shall we and so let us so also bear the image [of the Man] of heaven* (1 Corinthians 15:45-49 AMP).

As a mountain mover, I do not see myself as a mere mortal. I am a supernatural child of God Almighty, operating with my Father's DNA, ready to accomplish on earth that which He has assigned me. Consistent with this teaching, Numbers 13:30-33 illustrates how the children of Israel, God's chosen people, were not victorious because of the way they perceived themselves.

Having a poor self-image was not the problem of the Israelites; it was having a poor image of who they were in the Lord.

> *And Caleb stilled the people before Moses, and said, Let us go up at once, and possess it; for we are well able to overcome it. But the men that went up with him said, We be not able to go up against the people; for they are stronger than we. And they brought up an evil report of the land which they had searched unto the children of Israel, saying, The Land, through which we have gone to search it, is a land that eateth up the inhabitants thereof; and all the people that we saw in it are men of great stature. And there we saw the giants, the sons of Anak, which come of the giants: and we were in our own sight as grasshoppers, and so we were in their sight.* (Numbers 13:30-33)

God promised the Israelites the land of Canaan was theirs to possess, yet they wandered in the desert for forty years. The children of Israel did not see themselves as God's chosen people covered by the supernatural power of the Holy Spirit; they visualized themselves as mere grasshoppers. How do you perceive yourself in the midst of standing before mountains that seem unmovable?

Called by God as a female in ministry, I had to learn not to be intimidated by those who confronted me with such statements as "God does not use women to preach His word, lead His people or teach men." I specifically remember one gentleman saying to me, "I don't believe in women preachers or agree with what you are doing." Trying not to be sarcastic, I responded, "People do not believe in Hell either, but there is one." Once the Lord demonstrated His thoughts for me through His word, showing me how He utilized mighty women of God to accomplish His will, I refused to allow anyone other than my Creator tell me what I was predestined to become. I now know that I have a rich inheritance in the Lord in this life and the life to come.

Another example of one suffering from an identity crisis can be found in the parable of the lost son in Luke 15:17-22. Like Adam in the Garden of Eden (Genesis 3:1-7), the younger son in this parable was not satisfied with his present state of existence, one in which he had everything already prepared for him by his father. In his plight to enjoy the follies of the world, the young lad removed himself from the covering, of his father. Ending up in a distraught condition of embarrassment, the young man could no longer envision himself as a son of his father. In fact, he was willing to place himself in a position as a servant in his father's house if he was allowed to return home. The loving father would not permit his son to live the rest of his life as a house servant, but instead placed a robe and a ring upon his son symbolizing he was completely restored:

> *Then when he came to himself, he said, How many hired servants of my father have enough food, and [even food] to spare, but I am perishing (dying) here of hunger! I will get up and go to my father, and I will say to him, Father I have sinned against heaven and in your sight. I am no longer worthy to be called your son; [just] make me like one of your hired servants. So he got up and came to his [own] father. But while he was still a long way off, his father saw him and was moved with pity and tenderness [for him]; and he ran and embraced him and kissed him [fervently]. And*

the son said to him, Father, I have sinned against heaven and in your sight; I am no longer worthy to be called your son [I no longer deserve to be recognized as a son of yours]! But the father said to his bond servants, Bring quickly the best robe (the festive robe of honor) and put it on him; and give him a ring for his hand and sandals for his feet (Luke 15:17-22 *AMP*).

Through religious tradition, we have painted the wrong image of ourselves in the Lord. We say things like "I'm just an ol' sinner saved by grace." Are we still sinners, or are we new creations through the blood of our Lord and Savior, Jesus the Christ? We constantly speak of ourselves as servants or slaves of God, yet we do so with a sense of false humility. Many times we think of ourselves as hired servants, and not of serving our Father because we are His sons.

As a child, I can remember deacons of the church saying prayers that used statements such as "I'm Your poor, weak, humble servant." Most of these men never saw themselves as sons of God; therefore, they felt the need to beg—as undeserving slaves—when it came to making requests before the Lord. Through the lack of understanding sonship as a child of God, they felt they could not come boldly unto the throne of God to find mercy and grace in the time of need as stated in Hebrews 4:16. A more detailed explanation of sonship can be found in Romans 8:14-17a:

For all who are led by the Spirit of God are sons of God. For [the Spirit which] you have now received [is] not a spirit of slavery to put you once more in bondage to fear, but you have received the Spirit of adoption [the Spirit producing sonship] in [the

bliss of] which we cry, Abba (Father)! Father!
The Spirit Himself [thus] testifies together with
our own spirit, [assuring us] that we are children
of God. And if we are [His] children, then we are
[His] heirs also: heirs of God and fellow heirs
with Christ [sharing His inheritance with Him] ...
(AMP).

Until we see ourselves as sons of God with an inheritance and our Father's DNA, we will continue to appear powerless in situations we have already been given the power and authority to change. Not only have we been transformed from that defeated state caused by Adam's sin in the Garden of Eden, Ephesians 2:4-6 *AMP* testifies that we have been restored to our original place of authority through Christ our Lord:

But God—so rich is He in His mercy! Because of
and in order to satisfy the great and wonderful and
intense love with which He loved us, Even when
we were dead (slain) by [our own] shortcomings
and trespasses, He made us alive together in
fellowship and in union with Christ; [He gave us
the very life of Christ Himself, the same new life
with which He quickened Him, for] it is by grace
(His favor and mercy which you did not deserve)
that you are saved (delivered from judgment and
made partakers of Christ's salvation). And He
raised us up together with Him and made us sit
down together [giving us joint seating with Him]
in the heavenly sphere [by virtue of our being] in
Christ Jesus (the Messiah, the Anointed One).

Chapter 7
Operating As an Ambassador of Christ

So we are Christ's ambassadors, God making His appeal as it were through us. We [as Christ's personal representatives] beg you for His sake to lay hold of the divine favor [now offered you] and be reconciled to God.

2 Corinthians 5:20 *AMP*

According to the *Wikipeda Encyclopedia*, ambassadors are "ministers of the highest rank, with plenipotentiary authority to represent their head of state."[33] These ambassadors are expected to transact government business using the full power and authority they have been given by the headship they represent. Regardless of the foreign nations traveled, ambassadors are governed by their homeland, meaning they must submit themselves to the laws of their own country.

Second Corinthians 5:20 states that we as citizens of the Kingdom of Heaven are Christ's ambassadors on the earth. Christ came to earth representing God the Father and providing all who would receive an opportunity for full citizenship into the Kingdom of Heaven. The word "ambassador" applied in this scripture is interpreted from the word "*prĕsbĕuō*," meaning "Act as a representative."[34] As God's ambassador, Jesus was well aware that His sole purpose on earth was to do the will of His Father. In other words, Jesus only followed the pattern that was established by God in Heaven. Christ came to the earth bringing the government of God's Kingdom with Him:

For to us a Child is born, to us a Son is given; and

> *the government shall be upon His shoulder, and*
> *His name shall be called Wonderful Counselor,*
> *Mighty God, Everlasting Father [of Eternity],*
> *Prince of Peace. Of the increase of His government*
> *and of peace there shall be no end* (Isaiah 9:6-7a
> *AMP*).

A declaration by our Lord as to His mission on earth was given in John 6:38: *"For I came down from heaven, not to do mine own will, but the will of him that sent me."*

In like manner, as Christ's ambassadors, we must follow the pattern established by God as we represent His Kingdom on earth. Remember the message Jesus came to the earth proclaiming: *"Repent: for the kingdom of heaven is at hand."* We are told in Proverb 13: 17 *AMP*: *"A wicked messenger falls into evil, but a faithful ambassador brings healing."* This word "ambassador" translated from *"tsîyr"* [tseer] and is defined in the Hebrew dictionary as "a herald or errand-doer ..."[35] In the same scripture, the word "health" (KJV) or "healing" (*AMP*) is interpreted from the Hebrew word *"marpê"* (mar-pay'), meaning "a cure, deliverance, remedy..."[36] Jesus declared in Luke 4:18 that as an ambassador of God, He came to bring healing and deliverance to the world:

> *The Spirit of the Lord is upon me, because he*
> *hath anointed me to preach the gospel to the*
> *poor; he hath sent me to heal the broken hearted,*
> *To preach deliverance to the captives, and*
> *recovering of sight to the blind, to set at liberty*
> *them that are bruised, to preach the acceptable*
> *year of the Lord.*

Understanding that we have been restored to our place

of favor and authority through Jesus (Luke 4:19) and that we are Christ's ambassadors on the earth (2 Corinthians 5:20), as mountain movers we are commissioned by God to operate in the Power of His Spirit and bring a solution into our lives and the lives of others.

Returning to Genesis 1:3-4 *AMP*, let us examine the pattern established by God relative to functioning in His kingdom:

> *In the beginning God (prepared, formed, fashioned, and) created the heavens and the earth. The earth was without form and an empty waste, and darkness was upon the face of the very great deep. The Spirit of God was moving (hovering, brooding) over the face of the waters. And God said, Let there be light; and there was light. And God saw that the light was good (suitable, pleasant) and He approved it; and God separated the light from the darkness.*

Reading Genesis chapter one, we can conclude that everything the Father desired, He spoke forth and He saw that which He had spoken. Hebrews 4:12(a) declares that God's Word is powerful and alive, meaning it is active, operative and energizing. The same creative power was passed from God the Father, Son and Holy Ghost down to us. Remember the word "image" is defined as a phantom resemblance or representative. From the very beginning, God gave mankind the authority to operate in the same manner as Himself: *"And out of the ground the Lord God formed every beast of the field, and every fowl of the air; and brought them unto Adam to see what he would call them: and whatsoever Adam called every living creature, that was the name thereof"* (Genesis 2:19). Although God formed these animals, it was Adam's spoken word that declared what they should become. Adam's oneness with God (agreement with God) caused him to speak forth the intent of God.

John 1:1-3, 14 declares that Jesus Himself is God's Word made flesh and birthed upon the earth.

> *In the beginning [before all time] was the Word (Christ), and the Word was with God, and the Word was God Himself. He was present originally with God. All things were made and came into existence through Him; and without Him was not even one thing made that has come into being"(AMP).*

> *And the Word (Christ) became flesh (human, incarnate) and tabernacled (fixed His tent of flesh, lived awhile) among us; and we [actually] saw His glory (His honor, His majesty), such glory as an only begotten son receives from his father, full of grace (favor, loving-kindness) and truth" (AMP).*

Jesus recognized that all things came into existence by the Word of God and even though He was God, The Word, when He came to the earth it was still necessary to only speak forth that which had been ordained and instructed by the Father.

> *This is because I have never spoken of My own authority or of My own accord or as self-appointed, but the Father Who sent Me has Himself given Me orders [concerning] what to say and what to tell: And I know that His commandment is (means)*

eternal life. So whatever I speak, I am saying [exactly] what My Father has told Me to say and in accordance with His instructions (John 12:49 –50 *AMP*).

As I prepared this book, I hesitated to include so many scripture references. However, I realized that it is not my words that cause mountains to move; neither can my words be used to build faith. It is only the Word of our Lord, the King, that causes our faith to increase. Therefore, it is necessary for me to incorporate scripture to substantiate everything taught throughout this book.

This point is demonstrated even further in Matthew 16:19 when Christ gave us additional instructions as His ambassadors on the earth: *"I will give you the keys of the kingdom of heaven; and whatever you bind (declare to be improper and unlawful) on earth must be what is already bound in heaven; and whatever you loose (declared lawful) on earth must be what is already loosed in heaven" (AMP).* In other words, if it is not allowed in Heaven, we must not allow it on earth. If God permits it in Heaven, as His ambassadors we must permit or release it on the earth.

Matthew 6:10 reiterates this law of Heaven: *"Your kingdom come, Your will be done on earth as it is in heaven."* We must remember that the words we speak relative to ourselves have creative power because we are created in the image and after the likeness of God our Creator; therefore, what we speak should only testify of the will of Heaven.

The word "keys" applied in Matthew 16:19 originates from the Greek word *"klĕis"* [klice] meaning "a key as shutting a lock … metaphorically of 'the keys of the kingdom of heaven' which the Lord committed to Peter in Matthew 16:19, by which he would open the door of faith."[37] The door to overcoming limitless impossibilities is open to us as well when we operate as

Christ's ambassadors, speaking forth with the faith of God only those things that are permissible in Heaven. Moving mountains on command may seem impossible to some, but to a true ambassador of God, it is just another daily assignment.

Matthew 21:18-22 and Mark 11:12-24 record one of Jesus' demonstrations of the principle of using kingdom keys. Jesus and His disciples encountered a lone fig tree bearing leaves. The leaves indicated there also should have been figs. Jesus was hungry, and He went forth to the tree to partake of its fruit, except it was barren. In accordance with Genesis 1:11, God set order pertaining to fruit trees and vegetation and their ability to produce. It was unlawful according to the Kingdom of Heaven for the fig tree to be barren; therefore Jesus cursed the tree, and it dried up. Obviously, these words were spoken out loud because the disciples heard Jesus speak the curse upon the tree.

> *In the early dawn the next morning, as He was coming back to the city, He was hungry. And as He saw one single leafy fig tree above the roadside, He went to it but He found nothing but leaves on it [seeing that in the fig tree the fruit appears at the same time as the leaves]. And He said to it, Never again shall fruit grow on you! And the fig tree withered up at once. When the disciples saw it, they marveled greatly and asked How is it that the fig tree has withered away all at once? And Jesus answered them, Truly I say to you, if you have faith (a firm relying trust) and do not doubt, you will not only do what has been done to the fig tree, but even if you say to this mountain, Be taken up and cast into the sea, it will be done* (Matthew 21:18-21 *AMP*).

Reading throughout the four Gospels, many times Jesus spoke to situations, whether to storms, demons or disease. Through Matthew 21:21 and these other examples, it is clear that when we speak forth those things that are in accordance with the Laws of Heaven (the will of our Father and King), we will have whatever we say.

Proverbs 18:20-21 tells us *"A man's belly shall be satisfied with the fruit of his mouth; and with the increase of his lips shall he be filled. Death and life are in the power of the tongue: and they that love it shall eat the fruit thereof."* This same scripture is extrapolated in *The Amplified Bible* in this manner: *"A man's [moral] self shall be filled with the fruit of his mouth; and with the consequence of his words he must be satisfied [whether good or evil]. Death and life are in the power of the tongue, and they who indulge in it shall eat the fruit of it [for death or life]."*

Matthew 8:23-27 and Luke 8:22-25 both record an event where Jesus allowed His disciples to speak to their perilous situation. However, the little faith exemplified by Christ's disciples caused them to run to Him to be rescued. How many times have we run to the Lord in faithlessness when the ability to change the circumstances was on the tip of our tongues? The disciples should have considered the promises of Heaven.

Jesus stated to His disciples: *"Let us go over unto the other side of the lake"* (Luke 8:22b). It is obvious that Jesus had already purposed for them to reach the other side of the lake. In fact, none of them had fulfilled their purpose on the earth; therefore, it was unlawful according to Heaven for anything to cause their deaths at that time. This was an opportunity for the disciples to demonstrate their faith in the Word of God and their ability to represent Christ on the earth as His ambassadors. A mountain of fear stood between them and their victory.

A few summers ago, my daughter and son, Sharné and Christopher, set a fine example of our ability to change situations as Christ's ambassadors on the earth. They had been saving money for weeks so they could visit a local water park in our hometown of Decatur, Alabama. Our children had meticulously scheduled this event because of their busy summer. As the events of their special day unfolded, it became apparent that Sharné and Christopher were being subjected to a great lesson on stewardship and faith. As they prepared to leave for the water park, all three local television stations predicted heavy thunderstorms. Instead of Sharné, Christopher and their friends becoming frustrated or disappointed, they recalled the verses found in Matthew and Luke. Sharné and Christopher in agreement with Heaven spoke to the storms and the rain. The sun came out and they enjoyed their long awaited day at Point Mallard Park.

Our local newspaper reported this incident in an article about prayer because God had uniquely set up a newspaper interview for our church that same day. When the reporter covering another story mentioned to me about how surprised she was that we did not receive all the rain and thunderstorms predicted for the day, I shared our children's testimony with her. She reported the incident to another writer at the newspaper, and he included it in one of his articles. God always gets the glory!

Now is the time for us to operate as those supernatural beings God created. Those mountains or obstacles are waiting on us to speak to them in faith with the authority that has been given to us as ambassadors of our Lord.

Chapter 8
Confessions of a Mountain Mover

Truly I tell you, whoever says to this mountain, Be lifted up and thrown into the sea! and does not doubt at all in his heart but believes that what he says will take place, it will be done for him.

Mark 11: 23 *AMP*

It is not enough for us to know that we are Christ's ambassadors or that we have the God-given ability to move mountains; it is time we use the creative power of our words by faith and command those mountains to move. Previously in chapter two of this book, we discussed it is only by hearing the Word of God that our faith matures or increases. We also ascertained that we hear our own words more than those of anyone else. Unfortunately, we have heard ourselves speak death by making statements such as these instead of the life giving Word of God: "My head is killing me"; "I can't do this"; "I'm not going to make it"; "I don't have enough."

Proverbs 13:3 *AMP* reiterates this truth: *"He who guards his mouth keeps his life, but he who opens wide his lips comes to ruin."*

The significance of the words we speak can also be seen in the warning of judgment written in Matthew 12:36-37 *AMP*: *"But I tell you, on the day of judgment men will have to give account for every idle (inoperative, nonworking) word they speak. For by your words you will be justified and acquitted, and by your words you will be condemned and sentenced."*

In Hebrews 4:14, we are instructed to faithfully confess the words of our Lord: *"Seeing then that we have a great high priest, that is passed into the heavens, Jesus the Son of God, let us hold fast our profession."* The word "profession" according to the Greek dictionary is translated from the word *"hŏmŏlŏgia"* [hom-ol-og-ee'ah] and is defined as "acknowledgment: confession, profession."[38] *"Hŏmŏlŏgia"* as applied in verse fourteen is derived from the word *"hŏmŏlŏgĕō,"* meaning "to speak the same thing."[39] The two root words for these words are *"hŏmŏu"* [hom-oó], signifying "… at the same place or time"[40] and *"lŏgŏs"* [log'-os], "something said (including the thought)."[41] This definition of *lŏgŏs* reiterates that we hear our thoughts as well as the words we speak or read silently.

Our words, spoken or thought, must be identical with the Word of God, our King. Remember, we represent the Lord on the earth and anything said or thought contradictory to what God has spoken is poisonous to the foundation of our belief system and a misrepresentation of the Kingdom of Heaven. *"It is not what goes into the mouth of a man that makes him unclean and defiled, but what comes out of the mouth; this makes a man unclean and defiles [him]"* (Matthew 15:11 *AMP*).

Some believers have said that confessing God's Word daily aloud is unnecessary. However, according to Psalm 1:1-2, it is the only way to live successfully as a citizen of the Kingdom of Heaven.

BLESSED (HAPPY, fortunate, prosperous, and enviable) is the man who walks and lives not in the counsel of the ungodly [following their advice, their plans and purposes], nor stands [submissive and inactive] in the path where sinners walk, nor sits down [to relax and rest] where the scornful [and the mockers] gather. But his delight and desire are in the law of the Lord, and on His law (the precepts, the instructions, the teachings of God) he habitually meditates (ponders and studies) by day and by night (AMP).

Confessing the Word of God with the faith of God is the driving force to moving any mountain in our lives. Each Kingdom Word spoken is a driving force that breaks away at the foundation of those stubborn circumstances until they are moved from our God-given path.

For the Word that God speaks is alive and full of power [making it active, operative, energizing, and effective]; it is sharper than any two-edged sword, penetrating to the dividing line of the breath of life (soul) and [the immortal] spirit, and of joints and marrow [of the deepest parts of our nature]... (Hebrews 4:12 *AMP*).

God's Word not only separates man's spirit from the soul, but it is also the creator and sustainer of all things (Genesis 1:3-4,6-7 *AMP*; Hebrews 1:3 *AMP*; John 1:1-3 *AMP*). The Word of God is the only word that should be spoken in any situation or circumstance we may face.

When my husband and I first started New Genesis Community Church, a great mountain of lack (resources for ministry, personnel, etc.) seemed to stand between God's will and us. We used the Word of the Kingdom as our motivator instead of allowing circumstances to discourage us. *"And my God will liberally supply (fill to the full) your every need according to His riches in glory in Christ Jesus"* (Philippians 4:19 *AMP*). We knew we had been faithful in tithing and giving offerings; therefore, we were assured that the present situation had to change and line up with the Word of God. Confessing the promises of God along the way, Bishop and I continued to go forth with the plans God had given us, and daily, new provisions for the ministry materialized. Years later, we continue to stand on the promises of God's Word regardless of the opposition because we know God has already established our final outcome. Bishop Sam and I remind ourselves that God always makes provision for the vision He has given us.

It may seem unnatural or awkward at first to speak the language of Heaven instead of what is spoken around us by the world. Nevertheless, the more we speak God's Word about our challenges, the more habit-forming it will become. " ...*For out of the fullness (overflow, the superabundance) of the heart the mouth speaks*" (Matthew 12:34 *AMP*).

Recognizing the need to speak only that which is spoken by God, I asked the Holy Spirit to quicken me when I said or thought anything contrary to what God has said about me or my circumstances. *"Set a watch, O Lord, before my mouth: keep the door of my lips"* (Psalm 141:3). I knew I needed to see myself in the scripture so that I would be constantly reminded that I am a new creation in Christ. "I am delivered" (1John 5:4-5); "I am healed" (Isaiah 53:5); "All my needs are met according to God's riches in Glory by Christ Jesus" (Philippians 4:19).

During further study, the Lord drew my attention to the scripture found in Romans 10:10 *AMP*: *"For with the heart a person believes (adheres to, trusts in, and relies on Christ) and so is justified (declared righteous, acceptable to God), and with the mouth he confesses (declares openly and speaks out freely his faith) and confirms [his] salvation."* Researching this passage of scripture in greater detail, I realized I was not just acknowledging

Christ as my Savior for new birth and kingdom citizenship. It became apparent that every time I opened my mouth and confessed those things in my heart relative to Heaven's constitution (The Bible), I was speaking forth my freedom.

The word "confession" applied in Romans 10:10 is translated the same as the word "*hŏmŏlŏgia*" found in Hebrews 4:14. The word "salvation" is interpreted from the Greek word "*sōtēria,*" when means "deliverance, preservation ... material and temporal deliverance from danger and apprehension ... health."[42]

Another significant example of the power of our words can be found in Genesis 27:1-41. Through an act of deception, Isaac, the father of Esau and Jacob, spoke the blessing meant for his elder son Esau over his younger son Jacob. Although his wife Rebekah and his son Jacob had deceived Isaac, his words were irrevocable:

> *So he came near and kissed him; and [Isaac] smelled his clothing and blessed him and said, The scent of my son is as the odor of a field which the Lord has blessed. And may God give you of the dew of the heavens and of the fatness of the earth and abundance of grain and [new] wine; Let peoples serve you and nations bow down to you; be master over your brothers, and let your mother's sons bow down to you. Let every one be cursed who curses you and favored with blessings who blesses you. As soon as Isaac had finished blessing Jacob and Jacob was scarcely gone out from the presence of Isaac his father, Esau his brother came in from his hunting. Esau had also prepared savory food and brought it to his father and said to him, Let my father arise and eat of his*

*son's game, that you may bless me. And Isaac his
father said to him, Who are you? And he replied,
I am your son, your firstborn, Esau. Then Isaac
trembled and shook violently, and he said, Who?
Where is he who has hunted game and brought
it to me, and I ate of it all before you came and
I have blessed him? Yes, and he shall be blessed*
(Genesis 27: 27-33 *AMP*).

Sadly, the blessing intended for Esau fell on the life of
Jacob. In an attempt to retrieve that which he had been robbed of,
Esau pleaded with his father to bless him also. In Genesis 27:34-
38, the obvious agony felt in Esau's heart is demonstrated as he
realizes the words of his father has set the course of their lives.

*When Esau heard the words of his father, he cried
out with a great and bitter cry and said to his father,
Bless me, even me also, O my father! [Isaac]
said, Your brother came with crafty cunning and
treacherous deceit and has taken your blessing.
[Esau] replied, Is he not rightly named Jacob,
[the supplanter]? For he has supplanted me these
two times: he took away my birthright, and now
he has taken away my blessing! Have you not still
a blessing reserved for me? And Isaac answered
Esau, Behold, I have made [Jacob] your lord and
master; I have given all his brethren to him for
servants, and with corn and [new] wine have I
sustained him. What then can I do for you, my
son?* (Genesis 27:34-37 *AMP*).

Centuries later, the hatred stirred because of what Isaac

spoke over his two sons caused much bloodshed. The Amalekites, descendents of Esau, were the first enemies of the Israelites who fled Egypt. These Israelites were descendents of Jacob. *"Then came Amalek [descendants of Esau] and fought with Israel at Rephidim"* (Exodus 17: 8 *AMP*).

Many parents have yet to realize the words they say to their children hold much power. For years they speak curses instead of blessings over their children. The results of their words manifest in the lives of their children five to ten years later. These parents are oblivious as to why their children's behavior or lives result in such disappointment.

> *"And the tongue is a fire. [The tongue is a] world of wickedness set among our members, contaminating and depraving the whole body and setting on fire the wheel of birth (the cycle of man's nature), being itself ignited by hell (Gehenna)... But the human tongue can be tamed by no man. It is a restless (undisciplined, irreconcilable) evil, full of deadly poison. With it we bless the Lord and Father, and with it we curse men who were made in God's likeness!* (James 3: 6, 8-9 *AMP*)"

The blood of Jesus (Christ's redemptive act on the cross) and the Word of God (God's blessing on our lives) are the only remedy for these generational curses. *"Christ purchased our freedom [redeeming us] from the curse (doom) of the Law [and its condemnation] by [Himself] becoming a curse for us, for it is written [in the Scriptures], Cursed is everyone who hangs on a tree (is crucified)"* (Galatians 3:13 *AMP*).

As a parent seeking to direct our children toward their God-given destinies, I remember speaking words of life over our young son, Christopher. I constantly reminded him he was a mighty man of God. At around two-years-old, those traits began to manifest. One day when Christopher and I were playing in our front yard, our next-door neighbor called Christopher a cute little boy. Christopher innocently replied, "I'm a man of God; I'm a man of God." Those very thoughts of who he is in the Lord continue to remain fixed in Christopher's mind.

Recognizing the importance of the confessions of a mountain mover, I make it a point now to speak the words of the Kingdom of Heaven. These words are so embedded in my heart that I am disturbed to hear anything else spoken by or around me. You may be asking "What are the confessions of a mountain mover?" My response to that question is simple: every promise given to us in the Word of God. There are far too many promises from our King to list them all in the contents of this book. However, I have included a few of the confessions I speak forth to remind myself of who I am in Christ. As a supernatural mountain mover, this can be a wonderful place for you to begin speaking forth in faith. King David says in Psalm 19:14 *AMP, "Let the words of my mouth and the meditation of my heart be acceptable in Your sight, O Lord, my [firm, impenetrable] Rock and my Redeemer."*

The confessions below are paraphrased and I have included scriptures as references:

> *I am God's workmanship created for good works that my Father has predestined for me to do. Ephesian 2:10*
>
> *I am a son of God. John 1:12*
>
> *I am a friend of God. John 15:15*

I was bought with a great price; therefore in Christ my life is priceless. 2 Corinthians 6:20

I am an ambassador of the Kingdom of Heaven. 2 Corinthians 5:20

I hearken to the voice of the Lord; therefore, I am blessed when I go in and come out. My children (physical and spiritual) are blessed. All the works of my hands are blessed. My storehouses or bank accounts are blessed. All my enemies are smitten before me. I am a lender and not a borrower. I am above only and never beneath or on the bottom. Deuteronomy 28: 1-12

I am hidden in the secret place of God; therefore no disaster shall come near my dwelling. No sickness or disease shall cause sudden or premature death upon me. In my ways of obedience, God's angels protect me from hurt or harm. A thousand may fall at my side, even ten thousand at my right side, but in the hour of terrorism or any natural disaster, no harm shall come near my family or me. Psalm 91

By the stripes or wounds of Jesus I am healed; therefore, neither sickness nor disease shall reign in my body. Isaiah 53:5

I have authority and power to trample upon serpents and scorpions (Satan and his imps);

therefore nothing shall harm me. Luke 10:19

I am seated with Christ Jesus in heavenly places; therefore I am not confounded by circumstances on the earth. I make my observations from above knowing that through Christ I am victorious. Ephesians 2:6, 1 Corinthians 15:57

PRINCIPLE THREE
YOU MUST BELIEVE

Chapter 9
Seeing Is Not Believing

And Jesus said, [You say to Me], If You can do anything? [Why,] all things can be (are possible) to him who believes!

Mark 9:23 *AMP*

In addition to having the faith of God and holding fast to our confessions of the Word of God, as mountain movers we must have the capacity to believe that God's Word spoken through us possesses the same creative power as our Lord. *"Truly I tell you, whoever says to this mountain, Be lifted up and thrown into the sea! and does not doubt at all in his heart, but believes that what he says will take place, it will be done for him"* (Mark 11:23 *AMP*).

The word "believe" is translated from the Greek word *"pistĕuō"* [pist-yoo´-o], meaning "not just to believe, but also to be persuaded of; and hence to place confidence in, to trust, and signifies, in this sense of the word, reliance upon not mere credence, hence it is translated 'commit unto,' 'commit to one's trust,' 'be committed unto,' etc."[43] *"Pistĕuō"* is derived from the same Greek word as *"pistis,"* used to define faith. However, in this particular text, we are required by the Lord to believe that when we speak God's Word as His ambassador on the earth, we will witness the same results as Christ because we are His body on the earth:

I assure you, most solemnly I tell you, if anyone steadfastly believes in Me, he will himself be

> *able to do the things that I do: and he will do*
> *even greater things than these, because I go to*
> *the Father. And I will do [I Myself will grant]*
> *whatever you ask in My Name [as presenting all*
> *that I Am], so that the Father may be glorified*
> *and extolled in (through) the Son* (John 14:12-13
> *AMP*).

I am sure that a religious bone just shook in the lives of some of you reading this book because you think we do not have that kind of power or authority. Have you already forgotten who you are? Luke 6:40 will ease your thoughts of heresy relative to this teaching: "*A pupil is not superior to his teacher, but everyone [when he is] completely trained (readjusted, restored, set to rights, and perfected) will be like his teacher (AMP).*" Christ dying on the cross has restored us. As a result, the Holy Spirit is our Teacher and as His pupils, we are daily transitioning towards perfection in the Lord. Yes, we are in training and we are challenged when those mountains and obstacles stand before us. Will we pass the test by speaking boldly in faith to move those mountains, or will we cry to the Lord as His disciples did because they were fretful of perishing (Mark 4:35-40)?

Mark 11:23-24 shifts from speaking to the mountains to making prayer requests. The word "believe" is mentioned again in verse 24 when we are told that we must trust that the answer is granted to us when the request is made, not when we see it with our physical eyes. I have heard through televisions commercials, movies and the mouths of those who do not understand kingdom principles, "Seeing is believing." Modern visual technologies make this statement false even for the worldly system. You cannot believe everything you see. The only thing that is absolute in this world is God, His Word, His Power and His Presence. He is the final authority for those who believe.

In 2 Corinthians 5:7 *AMP*, we are reminded that our journey on earth is definitely a stride of faith: *"For we walk by faith [we regulate our lives and conduct ourselves by our conviction or belief respecting man's relationship to God and divine things, with trust and holy fervor; thus we walk] not by sight or appearance."*

Unlike Thomas in John 20:24-29, we must not rely on our natural senses to verify what has been promised to us by God. Following Christ's resurrection, Thomas was not present at a meeting between Jesus and His disciples. When the disciples reported to Thomas that the Lord had risen from the dead, Thomas responded in disbelief because he had not seen the Lord with his own eyes. He had no physical evidence; therefore, he chose not to believe.

> *But Thomas, one of the Twelve, called the Twin, was not with them when Jesus came. So the other disciples kept telling him, We have seen the Lord! But he said to them, Unless I see in His hands the marks made by the nails and put my finger into the nail prints, and put my hand into His side, I will never believe [it]. Eight days later His disciples were again in the house, and Thomas was with them. Jesus came, though they were behind closed doors, and stood among them and said, Peace to you! Then He said to Thomas, Reach out your finger here, and see My hands; and put out your hand and place [it] in My side. Do not be faithless and incredulous, but [stop your unbelief and] believe! Thomas answered Him, My Lord and my God! Jesus said to him, Because you have seen Me, Thomas, do you now believe (trust,*

*have faith)? Blessed and happy and to be envied
are those who have never seen Me and yet have
believed and adhered to and trusted and relied on
Me* (John 20:24-29 *AMP*).

There are three important observations we must note in
this particular incident. First, choosing to believe is an act of our
will. Thomas declared in verse 25, *"Except I see in his hands the
print of the nails and put my finger into the print of the nails, and
thrust my hand into his side, I will not believe."* Secondly, we
are pleasing to our Lord when we place complete confidence and
trust in Him without seeing the physical evidence of an answered
prayer. Finally, we are rewarded (*"Blessed, happy and to be
envied..."*) because we choose to believe what God has promised
regardless of any physical evidence.

How does our belief system evolve from living by what
we see to living by what God has said? From Adam's fall until
Christ's reintroduction of the Kingdom of God on the earth
(Matthew 4:17), the kingdom of darkness prevailed in the world.
Those things that were seen with the natural eye or through man's
intellect established mankind's belief system instead of absolute
trust in God:

*But Jesus loudly declared, The one who believes
in Me does not [only] believe in and trust in and
rely on Me, but [in believing in Me he believes]
in Him Who sent Me. And whoever sees Me sees
Him Who sent Me. I have come as a Light into the
world, so that whoever believes in Me [whoever
cleaves to and trusts in and relies on Me] may
not continue to live in darkness* (John 12: 44-46
AMP).

The word "darkness" used in John 12:46 is derived from the Greek word "*skŏtŏs*" meaning "intellectual darkness" or ..."moral and spiritual darkness."[44] Our thoughts before our rebirth into the Kingdom of God reflected darkness and ignorance.

Let the wicked forsake his ways and the unrighteous man his thoughts; and let him return to the Lord, and He will have love, pity, and mercy for him, and to our God, for He will multiply to him His abundant pardon. For My thoughts are not your thoughts, neither are your ways My ways, says the Lord. For as the heavens are higher than the earth, so are My ways higher than your ways and My thoughts than your thoughts (Isaiah 55:7-9 *AMP*).

As kingdom citizens, our sense of sight and man's opinions must not be the sources of the foundation for our belief system. The Word of God must establish our belief system; this produces faith. It is through the realm of the Spirit that we believe. Remember, the domain of our government, the Kingdom of Heaven, extends far beyond what can be seen with the natural eye.

Asked by the Pharisees when the kingdom of God would come, He replied to them by saying, The kingdom of God does not come with signs to be observed or with visible display, Nor will people say, Look! Here [it is]! or, See, [it is] there! For behold, the kingdom of God is within you [in your hearts] and among you [surrounding you]. (Luke 17: 20-21 *AMP*)

Many disciples who originally followed Christ eventually fell away from Him because they were seeking an earthly kingdom to overtake the governing authorities and authenticate Jesus' authority on the earth. However, Jesus made it clear to these "would be" followers that the ability to believe in Him had to be a walk of faith:

> It is the Spirit Who gives life [He is the Life-giver]; the flesh conveys no benefit whatever [there is not profit in it]. The words (truths) that I have been speaking to you are spirit and life. But [still] some of you fail to believe and trust and have faith. For Jesus knew from the first who did not believe and had no faith and who would betray Him and be false to Him. And He said, This is why I told you that no one can come to Me unless it is granted him [unless he is enabled to do so] by the Father. After this, many of His disciples drew back (returned to their old associations) and no longer accompanied Him (John 6:63-66 AMP).

Many who are saved do not experience the benefits of kingdom citizenship because we have not sought the Word of God for mind renewal. We choose to believe the worst possible scenario will manifest in our lives (based on the world system or the logistics of man) instead of expecting the blessings promised by God. We automatically disbelieve the impossible, yet when some of us speak negatively, we believe with surety those horrific situations will come forth. I must confess, I once thought this way. Thank God my spiritual eyes have been opened to the truth of

God's Word. The transformation of our minds to expect God's blessings is vital.

Written in Mark 9:23, Jesus informed a man with an epileptic son that belief in Him was the gateway to all impossibilities: *"Jesus said unto him, If thou canst believe, all things are possible to him that believeth."* The Amplified Bible translation of Mark 9:23 makes it clear that experiencing the impossible rests upon us and our ability to believe what God has said.

For some of us, the problem is not a matter of trusting the Lord, but trusting that what we seek from the Lord is what He desires for us. In those instances, James 1:5-8 is key to understanding that once God has made apparent His plans for us, we must not allow doubt to fester in our minds. Even when we do not see the results immediately, our position must be to stand in faith and believe that what we have said shall come to past:

> *If any of you is deficient in wisdom, let him ask of the giving God [Who gives] to everyone liberally and ungrudgingly, without reproaching or faultfinding, and it will be given him. Only it must be in faith that he asks with no wavering (no hesitating, no doubting). For the one who wavers (hesitates, doubts) is like the billowing surge out at sea that is blown hither and thither and tossed by the wind. For truly, let not such a person imagine that he will receive anything [he asks for] from the Lord, [For being as he is] a man of two minds (hesitating, dubious, irresolute), [he is] unstable and unreliable and uncertain about everything [he thinks, feels, decides]* (James 1: 5-8 *AMP*).

At the beginning of my tenth year as a civilian government employee, my heart ignited with a strong desire to remain home with our children. Our daughter Sharne' was five years old and our son Christopher was a newborn. During this season in our lives, my salary as an engineer was twice as much as my husband's. Outside of the fact that my husband and I had to be in agreement with me quitting my job, my greatest apprehension was being sure doing so was the absolute will of God for my life at this time. I strongly believed my place of employment was not just a means for additional income. I knew I had been placed there to be a light for Christ in the workplace. I needed confirmation I had made contact with everyone the Lord intended. Once I was assured the time in our lives was right for change and I knew it was God who planted that desire in my heart, I remained steadfast concerning God's promises of provision.

There were many who questioned my desire, yet I remained firm in what I knew the Lord had spoken to me. The situation seemed somewhat impossible because the Lord clearly said I would become an at-home mom the first of October. Our family's health insurance was provided through my job. I needed to give two weeks' notice because I was expected to return from maternity leave the week of October 1. Finally, my husband needed to feel assured this was what we needed to do.

True to His Word, the Lord worked out every circumstance, including new health insurance benefits through my husband's job effective October 1 of that year, an understanding supervisor who chose not to require a two weeks' notice, and a husband who decided that doing the will of God requires great faith.

Choosing to believe God is an act of our will. This may be the most difficult challenge for us as kingdom citizens, yet knowing that all things become possible to us when we believe is the ultimate incentive. It may look like you are facing defeat with two strikes, two outs and your worst hitter at bat, but nothing is impossible with God. What will you say to your situation? The Book of Job says it best: *"You shall also decide and decree a thing, and it shall be established for you; and the light [of God's favor] shall shine upon your ways"* (Job 22:28 *AMP*).

Chapter 10
The Dangers of Unbelief

And they were offended in him. But Jesus said unto them, A prophet is not without honour, save in his own country, and in his own house. And he did not many mighty works there, because of their unbelief.
Matthew 13:57-58

As kingdom citizens, our ultimate desire should be to please the Lord our King. According to Hebrews 11:6, it is impossible to please God without living by an absolute trust in His Word. *"But without faith it is impossible to please him: for he that cometh to God must believe that he is, and that he is a rewarder of them that diligently seek him."* If we are rewarded for living by absolute trust in God, we must know that a lifestyle of unbelief can halt the plans of God for our lives. *"Take heed, brethren, lest there be in any of you an evil heart of unbelief, in departing from the living God"* (Hebrews 3:12).

Hebrews 4:3 informs us that God has prepared a place of rest and worry-free living for those who believe or live by faith:

> *For we who have believed (adhere to and trusted in and relied on God) do enter that rest, in accordance with His declaration that those [who did not believe] should not enter when He said, As I swore in My wrath, They shall not enter My rest; and this He said although [His] works had been completed and prepared [and waiting for all who would believe] from the foundation of the*

world (AMP).

The children of Israel forfeited their part in this restful state of existence because of their lack of trust in the promises of God (Numbers 14:1-35; Hebrews 3:8– 4:10). They would have enjoyed a lifestyle similar to their Sabbath Day's rest if they had exhibited complete trust in the Lord.

> *So we see that they were not able to enter [into His rest], because of their unwillingness to adhere to and trust in and rely on God [unbelief had shut them out]. THEREFORE, WHILE the promise of entering His rest still holds and is offered [today], let us be afraid [to distrust it], lest any of you should think he has come too late and has come short of [reaching] it* (Hebrews 3:19 - 4:1 *AMP*).

The book of Genesis chapter one informs us that God created for six days and on the seventh day He rested. Everything we will ever need in the Lord was completed in those six days. In Hebrews 4:9-11 *AMP*, our Lord's rest on the seventh day symbolizes our restful existence as we place absolute trust in the Father. We do not have to work for what has already been paid for through Christ our Lord:

> *So then, there is still awaiting a full and complete Sabbath rest reserved for the [true] people of God; For he who has once entered [God's] rest also has ceased from [the weariness and pain] of human labors, just as God rested from those labors peculiarly His own. Let us therefore be zealous and exert ourselves and strive diligently*

to enter that rest [of God, to know and experience it for ourselves], that no one may fall or perish by the same kind of unbelief and disobedience [into which those in the wilderness fell].

We are not bound by a particular Sabbath Day of worship as in the Old Testament; however, Habakkuk 2:4 and Romans 1:17 state: *"...the just shall live by faith."* The word "shall" denotes that living by faith is a command from God. Each day we should live a worshipful day of rest through faith in God our Father.

The Greek word *"apistia"* [ap-is-teé-ah], meaning "faithlessness or disobedience,"[45] is used to describe God's chosen people, Israel, and Jesus' family and countrymen as seen in Matthew 13:57-58 *AMP*:

And they took offense at Him [they were repelled and hindered from acknowledging His authority, and caused to stumble]. But Jesus said to them, A prophet is not without honor except in his own country and in his own house. And He did not do many works of power there, because of their unbelief (their lack of faith in the divine mission of Jesus).

Neither group of people received God's best for their lives because of unbelief. Clearly stated, faithlessness is considered an act of disobedience. After understanding the Word of God, what we hear must be united with absolute trust in God to bring us into our place of promise or destiny:

For indeed we have had the glad tidings [Gospel of God] proclaimed to us just as truly as they [the Israelites of old did when the good news of deliverance from bondage came to them]; but the message they heard did not benefit them, because it was not mixed with faith (with the leaning of the entire personality on God in absolute trust and confidence in His power, wisdom, and goodness) by those who heard it; neither were they united in faith with the ones [Joshua and Caleb] who heard (did believe) (Hebrews 4:2 *AMP*).

Re-examining the children of Israel in the wilderness, it was unbelief or lack of faith that caused them to remain wanderers for 40 years. The same principle applies in our lives today. Many are still wandering in "wilderness" experiences, expecting God to automatically move them forward. However, God's intervention will prevail only when faith is in operation by His people. The wilderness for the Israelites was a place of just enough provision on a daily basis. Yes, there were supernatural provisions, yet there were also limitations and tests by God. Those tests were to prove what was in their hearts: faith—or doubt and unbelief.

It is God's ultimate desire for us, as His children, to experience a free flowing, more-than-enough place of victory: a place where we live in an overflow of His presence and provisions. Consequently, faith (absolute trust in God and His promises) is the only thing that will move us from that wilderness experience into our Canaan or place of destiny.

Recapitulating Matthew 13:57-58, it was Jesus' desire to heal many in His hometown. I imagine that some of those who needed healing or deliverance were family or people who knew him well. However, their deliverance by the Lord was not possible because of their unbelief.

Consequently, we must not waiver in our faith as to

whether God will hear and answer the requests we have made. We cannot say we believe we receive the answer when we pray and then later try to systematically answer the prayer ourselves, seeking to guess God's next move. Neither can we allow our imaginations to overtake us with doubts or thoughts contrary to the answer God's Word has promised.

Second Corinthians 10:5-6 reminds us all our contrary thoughts or misgivings must be held captive to the obedience of Christ. *"Casting down imaginations, and every high thing that exalteth itself against the knowledge of God, and bringing into captivity every thought to the obedience of Christ; And having in a readiness to revenge all disobedience, when your obedience is fulfilled."* We must think according to the Word of God, not according to the things we see in the physical realm.

In a world that seeks physical evidence, we are required by God to place our complete trust and lives in the hands of One we cannot see. As an ambassador of God in a world that does not comprehend what true allegiance necessitates, I understand why it is so difficult for many of us to place ourselves in a position of such vulnerability. After all, previous to accepting Christ as our Lord and Savior, many of us felt that everything in our lives centered on our own thoughts and dreams; other than ourselves, there was no one we could place absolute trust in. Nevertheless, it is now time for us to come to the realization that because we are in a world that does not comprehend true commitment, we must anchor our hearts (trust) in a Mighty God whose kingdom and power transcends all of Heaven and the earth. We must seek to liberate ourselves from unbelief.

PRINCIPLE FOUR

EXPECT TO RECEIVE

Chapter 11
Learning to Receive

And whatever you ask for in prayer, having faith *and* [really] believing, you will receive.
Matthew 21:22 *AMP*

T he concept of receiving from the Lord or anyone else should be simple to comprehend. Yet, misguided thoughts of considering oneself undeserving along with other fallacies can hinder our ability to be the recipient of God's promises. How many times have we been offered a gift of appreciation for something we have done and refused it, as though it was not necessary? On many occasions, we respond to acts of kindness from others by saying, "You didn't have to do that"; "This wasn't necessary"; or "Oh, you shouldn't have done that!" Refusing to receive from others can be seen as a form of false humility, which is an enemy of those who should expect to receive from the Lord.

Throughout the Word of God, we have seen that for every action there is a reaction: seedtime and harvest (Genesis 8:22); give and it shall be given (Luke 6:38); believe and you shall receive (Mark 11:24). The word "receive" used in Mark 11:24 is translated from the Greek word "*lambanō*" (lam-ban´-o), meaning "to take, to get hold of…obtain."[46] According to this definition, we are obligated to take action. If we do not accept or receive what the giver offers, their acts of generosity become meaningless.

The most significant biblical example of giving and receiving can be found in Romans 10:9, which declares: *"That if thou shalt confess with thy mouth the Lord Jesus, and shalt believe in thine heart that God hath raised him from the dead, thou shalt be saved."* God's plan of salvation has already been prepared for all who choose to accept or receive it; salvation is offered to everyone. However, the reality of what God did for each of us occurs only when we personally receive this gift of His Son. The key is accepting God's generosity.

In a similar manner, all the promises of God have been prepared for us since the foundation of the world. Although these provisions exist, if we do not take possession of them as our own, these benefits remain untouched. The Word of God in Isaiah 53:5 states: *"But he was wounded for our transgressions, he was bruised for our iniquities: the chastisement of our peace was upon him; and with his stripes we are healed."* The provision for wholeness for our spirit, soul and body was made over 2000 years ago. However, it is up to each individual to believe and receive the healing virtue provided through Christ's suffering on the cross.

The words "believe" and "receive" have an important connection in the scripture. The Lord requires us to believe that His benefits are available for each of us to receive. Amazingly, I have experienced situations where I prayed with great faith for others, but when I faced similar situations, faith for myself was small. Mark 11:24 stresses that we must believe *we* receive the answer when we pray. Not only must we believe what God has said, we must believe that He has said it for each of us.

If you or I were the only ones left on earth, God's promises would still be available for us to receive. What happened during those times when my faith was small? I had allowed excuses from past failures or the misguided thought of not seeing myself as a deserving recipient hinder my ability to welcome God's answer to my prayer. After I studied the word of God pertaining to my issue and placed myself in the scripture, I was able to accept the promise of God for my deliverance.

Revisiting Jesus' hometown (Matthew 13:57-58),

His kindred and neighbors did not believe He was the Son of God; therefore they could not receive from Him. They allowed familiarity of Jesus' earthly background keep them from accepting the delivering power of His heavenly heritage. *"A prophet is not without honor except in his own country and in his own house"* (Matthew 13:57b *AMP*). There have been times when family members or those who knew me as a youth would not receive a word of knowledge or prophecy from me because they could not get past the familiarity of my local existence. My heart was heavy for them to receive what God was speaking through me. Nevertheless, it was their choice to welcome that promise from God for their lives.

In the early 1990s, a great hunger for God and His Word evolved within me. Led by the Holy Spirit, I began to study in depth the Book of Acts. I had not been educated about the Power of the Holy Spirit because of the church affiliation in which I grew up. Yet, I knew there was more to my relationship with God and His ability to do great things for and through me. I remember reading Acts 1:8: *"But you shall receive power (ability, efficiency, and might) when the Holy Spirit has come upon you ..."* (*AMP*). I knew the Holy Spirit was in me, but I desired to have His Power upon me—I desired the baptism of the Holy Spirit. As I studied, I realized it was a matter of absolute surrender to God, allowing Him to be in complete charge of my life.

Through the Word of God and other excellent books about the Holy Spirit, it became apparent that God's precious gift of the Holy Spirit was available to all who would receive Him. I recall telling the Lord that even though I did not understand everything about the Book of Acts at that time, whatever those people had, I wanted! The key was that I believed God's Word and I was willing to receive or welcome God's Power and presence in and upon my life. Are you willing to receive all that the Lord has for you?

Chapter 12
Faith or Hope: Is There a Difference?

"NOW FAITH is the substance of things hoped for, the evidence of things not seen."

Hebrews 11:1

Based on previous study, we have come to the understanding that faith is a constant, absolute trust in the Word of God. I use the word "constant" because we know that faith is always operative. Re-examining Hebrews 11:1, notice the word "hoped" used in this passage of scripture: *"NOW FAITH is the substance of things hoped for, the evidence of things not seen."* Many of us have used the words "hope" and "faith" interchangeably. However, a word study will reveal to us that these words differ. As previously stated, faith means having an absolute, unmovable trust in God and His promises. We have also established that because of faith, we believe we receive an answer from the Lord immediately, regardless of the physical evidence. No matter how the circumstances appear to us in the natural realm, we know that God's Word is the final authority in every situation.

The word "hoped" used in Hebrews 11:1 is translated from the word *"ĕlpizō"* [el-pid´-zo], meaning "to expect..."[47] This word *"ĕlpizō"* is derived from another word, *ĕlpis* [el-pec´], meaning "(to anticipate, usually with pleasure); expectation."[48] Hope actually *looks forward* with expectations of receiving in the physical realm that which has already been received by faith in the spirit realm.

An excellent biblical example of faith and hope can be found in Romans 4:18–21 (*AMP*):

[For Abraham, human reason for] hope being gone, hoped in faith that he should become the father of many nations, as he had been promised, So [numberless] shall your descendants be. He did not weaken in faith when he considered the [utter] impotence of his own body, which was as good as dead because he was about a hundred years old, or [when he considered] the barrenness of Sarah's [deadened] womb. No unbelief or distrust made him waiver (doubtingly question) concerning the promise of God, but he grew strong and was empowered by faith as he gave praise and glory to God.

Verse 18 conveys that regardless of Abraham's age and his physical inability to impregnate his wife, God still promised Abraham he would be the father of many nations. It further states in verse 19 that Abraham expected the fulfillment of the promise based on his faith (absolute trust in God and His promises) and not on the condition of his body or his wife's. The words "faith" and "hope" are not used interchangeably. In fact, we can see that faith is the substance that brings God's promises we anticipate from Heaven to us on the earth.

An example of prayer without expectations of an immediate answer from the Lord can be found in the twelfth chapter of Acts. The church of God was under severe persecution. King Herod had already executed James, the brother of John, and Peter was locked in prison awaiting his death as well. The saints of God had gathered at John's mother's house for prayer when God suddenly brought deliverance. In fact, those who prayed were startled by the outcome:

Then Peter came to himself and said, Now I really know and am sure that the Lord has sent His angel and delivered me from the hand of Herod and from all that the Jewish people were expecting [to do to me]. When he, at a glance, became aware of this [comprehending all the elements of the case], he went to the house of Mary the mother of John, whose surname was Mark, where a large number were assembled together and were praying. And when he knocked at the gate of the porch, a maid name Rhoda came to answer. And recognizing Peter's voice, in her joy she failed to open the gate, but ran in and told the people that Peter was standing before the porch gate. They said to her, You are crazy! But she persistently and strongly and confidently affirmed that it was the truth. They said, It is his angel! But meanwhile Peter continued knocking, and when they opened the gate and saw him, they were amazed (Acts 12:11-16 *AMP*).

According to Hebrews 11:1, there should always be an expectation of the physical manifestation of the request we have made to God; that is what the word "hope" means as it relates to our faith. Many times when we have used the words "faith" and "hope" interchangeably, we did not grasp the validity of anticipating a definite answer from God. In fact, there were scenarios when the word "hope" was taken out of its scriptural context because faith was not involved; the expectation was based on presumption. The word "hope" was used with double-minded thoughts: maybe God will, maybe He will not. This is mere speculation without any substance based on the Word of God to support an anticipated positive physical outcome.

It is our faith that gives us hope or an expectant observation for the glorious return of our Lord and Savior, Jesus Christ. Colossians 1:5-6a *AMP* tells us: *"Because of the hope [of experiencing what is] laid up (reserved and waiting) for you in heaven. Of this [hope] you heard in the past in the message of the truth of the Gospel, which has come to you."* This entire scripture speaks of the future and not the present. Galatians 5:5 articulates Christ's return in this manner: *"For we through the Spirit wait for the hope of righteousness by faith."* We are waiting with anticipation (hope) for Christ's return. However, it is faith (absolute trust in God and His Word) that gives us strength while we wait.

In the very same manner we anticipate the glorious return of our Lord and Savior, Jesus Christ, we must expect all the promises of God to be fulfilled in our lives. We must see the answer through the eyes of faith and stand on the Word of God, expecting the natural manifestation to come forth.

CONCLUSION

In Proverbs 11:9, we are told that a godless man can destroy his neighbor with his mouth, but the people of God are delivered through knowledge. In the preceding twelve chapters I have emphasized the knowledge provided by God's Word to transform us into mountain movers. Also, I have shared personal experiences where the application of these biblical truths caused mountains to move for me.

In retrospect, the mountains I have faced the past 25 years have drawn me closer to understanding who I am in Christ as well as how I must represent my Lord on this earth. No, I have not been confronted with some of the situations and circumstances that many others have been challenged by; however, the principles for overcoming these obstacles are the same. The solution to these many barriers blocking our paths is right under our noses. We must speak to the mountains instead of speaking about them.

What is the greatest hindrance standing between you and your destiny? It is your choice to have the faith of God, speak to the mountains, and believe and expect to receive what God has promised. It is my prayer that you will not allow past failures, depression, prejudices, socio-economic status or disease prevent you from going forth. Keep in mind, we are created in the image and after the likeness of our Father. We have His DNA (Divine Nature and Authority), and all things are possible to those who believe. Make a decision today and *SPEAK FORTH.*

Experiencing the Kingdom of God

Written in John 3:1-18 of the Bible, a Jewish leader named Nicodemus came to Jesus late one night to discuss the signs and wonders authenticating Jesus' ministry on the earth. The Lord's response to Nicodemus was an explanation of how he could partake of the wonders of the Kingdom of God as well: *"Jesus answered him, I assure you, most solemnly I tell you, that unless a person is born again (anew, from above), he cannot ever see (know, be acquainted with, and experience) the kingdom of God"* John 3:3 *AMP*.

Experiencing God's Kingdom includes having unbroken fellowship with God our Father eternally: *"For God so greatly loved and dearly prized the world that He [even] gave up His only begotten (unique) Son, so that whoever believes in (trusts in, clings to, relies on) Him shall not perish (come to destruction, be lost) but have eternal (everlasting) life"* John 3:16 *AMP*. How can this new birth begin for each of us? Romans 10:9 clearly states: *"That if thou shalt confess with thy mouth the Lord Jesus, and shalt believe in thine heart that God hath raised him from the dead, thou shalt be saved."*

If you are ready to experience everything God has provided for us in this life and in the life to come, please pray the following prayer:

> *Lord, I acknowledge that I have not included Your plans for me as part of my life. I also now realize I need a Savior to restore me back to a relationship with You. I therefore accept Your Son, Jesus, as my Redeemer. Please forgive me for my sins and restore my life in You. I ask you now to lead me to those you have assigned to teach me Your*

ways and how to further develop a meaningful relationship with You as my Lord. In the name of Jesus, I make this request to You. Amen

Please share your new life in Christ with others and consistently read the Word of God (The Bible) to increase your spiritual growth. Seek to follow God's directions as He connects you with a place of worship that will benefit your new life in Christ and lead you in the fulfillment of your God-given destiny.

About the Author

Dr. Yvette Rice ministers the gospel of Jesus Christ with a prophetic voice throughout the Body of Christ. In 2002, she assisted her husband, Bishop Sam Rice, Th.D., in establishing the New Genesis Community Church in Decatur, Alabama. Their mission in ministry is to proclaim the Gospel of Jesus Christ to the unsaved, the outcast, the bruised and the brokenhearted. Allowing the Gift of the Holy Spirit to work through her in the Fivefold Ministry, Dr. Rice seeks to empower the people of God to be faithful and effective as they fulfill God's Great Commission to proclaim the Kingdom Message of Christ to the lost.

In 2004, Dr. Rice established L.L.I.V.E. Ministry (Ladies Living In Victory and Excellence) at the New Genesis Community Church. Promoting life as an overcomer in Christ, many women have received deliverance, encouragement and greater stability in their walk with God through classes, WORD-shops and worship services provided by L.L.I.V.E. Ministry.

Dr. Rice and her husband, Bishop Sam Rice, Th.D., are the spiritual children of Apostle Maurice (Lady Brenda) Wright, Th.D., of the United Christian Church, Gadsden, Alabama. Bishop Sam and Pastor Yvette are in covenant fellowship with Apostle Halton (Elder Alicia) Horton of The Day Star Tabernacle - The 7000 More International Church Covenant Fellowship, Douglasville, Georgia.

A native of Decatur, Alabama, Dr. Yvette Rice has a bachelors of science degree in petroleum engineering from the University of Alabama at Tuscaloosa and holds a masters and doctorate degrees in theology from the North Carolina College of Theology. She is the proud mother of two wonderful children, Sharné and Christopher.

To contact Dr. Yvette Rice
write:

Dr. Yvette Rice
P.O. Box 1672
Decatur, AL 35602

Please include your prayer requests, comments and testimonials
when you write.

1 James Strong, "The New Strong's Expanded Dictionary of the Words in the Greek New Testament," in *The New Strong's Expanded Exhaustive Concordance of the Bible* (Nashville: Thomas Nelson Publishers, 2001), p.182, entry # 3735, s.v. "mountain," Matthew 21:21.

2 *Merriam - Webster's New College Dictionary* (Springfield, Massachusetts, U. S. A.: G. &C. Merriam Company, 1974), s.v. "ice cream."

3 Strong, "Greek," p. 202, entry #4102, s.v. "faith," Hebrews 11:1.

4 Strong, "Greek," p. 196, entry #3982, s.v. "persuaded," Romans 8:38.

5 Strong, "Greek," p.260, entry #5287, s.v. "substance," Hebrews 11:1.

6 Strong, "Greek," p.258, entry #5259, s.v. "under, through."

7 Strong, "Greek," p.163, entry #3358, s.v. "measure," Romans 12:3.

8 Strong, "Greek," p.252, entry #5118, s.v. "great," Matthew 8:10.

9 Strong, "Greek," p.158, entry #3173, s.v. "great," Matthew 15:28.

10 Strong, "Greek," p.177, entry #3640, s.v. "little faith," Matthew 6:30.

11   Strong, "Greek," p.162, entry #3339, s.v. "transform," Romans 12:2.

12   Strong, "Greek," p.11, entry #189, s.v. "hearing," Romans 10:17.

13   Strong, "Greek," p.12, entry #191, s.v. "hear," Mark 4:23.

14   Strong, "The New Strong's Expanded Dictionary of the Words in the Hebrew Bible," p. 66, entry #1897, s.v. "meditate," Joshua 1:8.

15   Strong, "Greek," p.79, entry #1537, s.v. "cometh," Romans 10:17.

16   Strong, "Greek," p.9, entry #154 and p. 219, entry # 441, s.v. "ask," Luke 11:9.

17   Strong, "Greek," p. 194, entry #3954, s.v. "boldly," Hebrews 4:16.

18   Strong, "Greek," p.9, entry #154, s.v. "request," Philippians 4:6.

19   Strong, "Greek," p.102, entry #2041, s.v. "work," James 2:21.

20   Strong, "Greek," p.2, entry #26, s.v. "love," Ephesians 6:23, 1 Corinthians 13, 1 John 4:18.

21   Merriam - Webster's, s.v. "presumption."

22   Merriam - Webster's, s.v. "probability."

23   Merriam - Webster's, s.v. "chance."

24   Merriam - Webster's, s.v. "presume."

25   *The New Open Bible*, New King James version (Nashville, Tenn.: Thomas Nelson Publishers, 1990), 1 The Old Testament.

26   Strong, "Greek," p.203, entry #4119, s.v. "excellent," Hebrews 11:4.

27   Strong, "Hebrew," p. 45, entry #1254, s.v. "created," Genesis1:1.

28   Strong, "Hebrew," p.221, entry #6213, s.v. "make," Genesis 1:26.

29   Strong, "Hebrew," p. 238, entry #6754, s.v. "image," Genesis 1:26.

30   Strong, "Hebrew," p. 64, entry #1823, s.v. "likeness," Genesis 1:26.

31   Strong, "Greek," p. 205, entry #4151, s.v. "Spirit," John 4:24.

32   Strong, "Greek," p.205, entry #4151, s.v. "spirit," 1 Thessalonians 5:23.

33   http://en.wikipedia.org/wiki/Ambassador (diplomacy), s.v. "ambassador."

34   Strong, "Greek," p. 209, entry #4243, s.v. "ambassador," 2 Corinthians 5:20.

35   Strong, "Hebrew," p. 238, entry #6735, s.v. "ambassador," Proverbs 13:17.

36   Strong, "Hebrew," p. 172, entry #4832, s.v. "health," Proverbs 13:17.

37   Strong. "Greek," p. 139, entry #2807, s.v. "keys," Matthew 16:19.

38   Strong. "Greek," p. 179, entry #3671, s.v. "profession," Hebrews 4:14.

39   Strong. "Greek," p. 179, entry #3670, s.v. "confess," Hebrews 4:14.

40   Strong. "Greek," p. 179, entry #3674, s.v. "same," Hebrews 4:14.

41   Strong. "Greek," p. 152, entry #3056, s.v. "word," Hebrews 4:14.

42   Strong, "Greek," p. 246, entry #4991, s.v. "salvation," Romans 10:10.

43   Strong, "Greek," p. 202, entry #4100, s.v. "believe," Mark 11:23.

44   Strong, "Greek," p. 227, entry #4655, s.v. "darkness," John 12:46.

45   Strong, "Greek," p.34, entry #570, s.v. "unbelief," Matthew 13:58.

46   Strong. "Greek." p.149, entry #2983, s.v. "receive," Mark 11:22.

47   Strong. "Greek" p.85, entry #1679, s.v. "hoped," Hebrews 11:1.

48   Strong. "Greek" p.85, entry #1680, s.v. "hope," Romans 4:18.

Made in the USA
Charleston, SC
30 May 2012